MAKING BABY'S CLOTHES

25 fun and practical projects for 0–3 year olds

ROB MERRETT

KT-376-657

CICO BOOKS

LONDON NEW YORK

To my soulmate, Luis

Published in 2010 by CICO Books
An imprint of Ryland Peters & Small Ltd
20–21 Jockey's Fields   519 Broadway, 5th Floor
London WC1R 4BW   New York, NY 10012

www.cicobooks.com

10 9 8 7 6 5 4 3 2 1

Text copyright © Rob Merrett 2010
Design and photography copyright © CICO Books 2010

The author's moral rights have been asserted. All rights reserved. No part of this publication may be reproduced, stored in a retrieval system, or transmitted in any form or by any means, electronic, mechanical, photocopying, or otherwise, without the prior permission of the publisher.

A CIP catalog record for this book is available from the Library of Congress and the British Library.

ISBN-13: 978 1 907030 70 3

Printed in China

Editor: Katie Hardwicke
Designer: Roger Hammond
Photographer: Julia Bostock except pages 6, 22l & r, 23l & r, 24–27, 32–37, 57c, 70–73, 100c, 101r, 114–121 by Vanessa Davies
Art direction and styling: Rob Merrett
Illustrator: Michael Hill

ACKNOWLEDGMENTS

I'd like to thank the following people for all their hard work and support over the past months: Julia Bostock and Vanessa Davies, for their adorable photographs; Michael Hill, for his many lovely illustrations; Katie Hardwicke, for her enthusiasm and keen editorial eye; Roger Hammond, for his great design; Pete Jorgensen, whom I'm sure I nearly drove "bonkers" during production, and Sally Powell, for arranging the models.

A special THANK YOU and BIG HUG go out to all my adorable models: Claudia, Elijah, Erin, Frankie, Grace, Harley, Kaye, Matilda, Okeri, Sid, and Zachary.

A big thank you to the location owners who welcomed us into their homes.

And, of course, thank you Mum, for encouraging me to sew and trying your very best to teach me to knit—unfortunately without much success.

Contents

Introduction

Extremely stylish baby clothes are easy to come by. In store or online, the choice is breathtaking and many designs for little ones have the same "must-have" appeal that we normally associate with adult designer fashion. They do, however, come at a price, often a very hefty one. And, more often than not, they also come heavily embellished with designer graphics and branded logos. Why spend a small fortune advertising a designer's label when you can create a "super-special," one-off wardrobe for your own or friend's children yourself for a fraction of the cost?

This book is filled with beautiful, boutique-quality outfits that are easy to make, guaranteed to turn heads, and simple to re-work in your child's favorite colors, fabrics, and print motifs. As the appeal of and demand for the "one-off," the "hand-crafted," and the "personalized" continues to grow in all areas of design and manufacturing—from cars to cupcakes, fragrance to furniture, parties to patios—this humble little book will provide you with the means to create a totally unique wardrobe that your child will love to wear.

The book is divided into chapters featuring garments suitable for different age ranges and you will find three pattern sizes for each project at the back of the book. The list of materials and fabric quantities given in the "You will need" list for each project are based on the pattern size for the featured garment, indicated in bold in the "Pattern sizes" list. Check the size chart below to establish the correct pattern size for your child. Hems and sleeve or pant lengths can easily be adjusted, and you can personalize your project from the wide choice of fabrics, embellishments, buttons, and trimmings that are available in store and online (see Suppliers, page 127).

With ready-to-trace patterns and clear step-by-step instructions, the projects are straightforward to make, whether you have basic dressmaking skills or are a seasoned seamstress. With a sewing machine and a little creative flair, you'll soon be dressing your little one in his or her own bespoke collection.

	0–3 months	3–6 months	6–9 months	9–12 months	2 years	3 years
chest	18½ in./47 cm	19¼ in./49 cm	20 in./51 cm	21 in./53 cm	22 in./56 cm	22½ in./57 cm
waist	17½ in./44 cm	18 in./46 cm	19 in./48 cm	19¾ in./50 cm	20½ in./52 cm	21 in./53 cm
height	24½ in./62 cm	27 in./68 cm	29 in./74 cm	31½ in./80 cm	36¼ in./92 cm	38½ in./98 cm

0–3 MONTHS

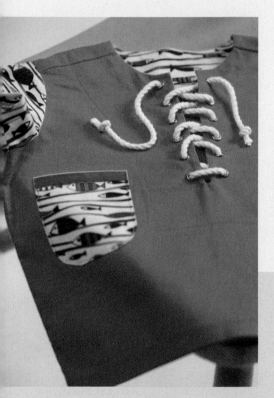

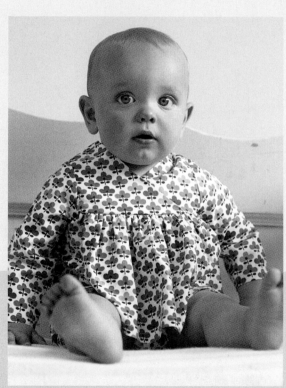

Flower Child
Gone Fishin'
Hello Petal!

Flower Child

This stylish dress can be finished in no time. The dainty button-trimmed placket and gentle gathers at the back neck are the only things that require a little extra care and attention. In an exuberant "Tropicana" floral print, this dress spells "summertime"—big time!—but it would work equally well in a classic stripe with a crisp, little white placket for a more discreet take on easy summer dressing.

1 Cut one front, two backs, and two 3 x 32¹/₄-in. (8 x 82-cm) strips for the hem flounce in the floral fabric. Apply lightweight interfacing to the wrong side of the piece of plain fabric and cut out one bib placket, using the template on the pull-out section.

2 Pin and baste (tack) a 10¹/₄-in. (26-cm) length of bias binding to the outer edge of the placket and stitch the binding in place (see page 125).

You will need

- Pattern A: front (A1) and back (A3)
- Bib placket template
- 17³/₄-in. (45-cm) piece of 45-in. (112-cm) wide floral fabric
- 3 x 4³/₄-in. (8 x 12-cm) piece of plain fabric in contrast color
- 3 x 4³/₄-in. (8 x 12-cm) piece of lightweight iron-on interfacing
- 137³/₄ in. (350 cm) bias binding, ¹/₂ in. (12 mm) wide
- Three x ¹/₂ in. (12 mm) diameter buttons
- Matching thread

Pattern sizes: 3, 6, and 9 months

Note: Take ³/₈-in. (1-cm) seam allowances throughout, unless otherwise stated

3 Place the placket in the center of the dress front, aligning the curved upper edges of the placket and the dress neck. Pin, baste (tack), and machine stitch in place, carefully topstitching alongside the inside edge of the bias binding.

4 Gather 2¹/₄ in. (6 cm) of the center back neck by hand or by machine to 1¹/₄ in. (3 cm), approximately ¹/₄ in. (5 mm) in from the raw edge (see page 122). Press the gathers flat.

5 Carefully bind the front and back neck edges with 7-in. (18-cm) lengths of bias binding, ensuring the top of the front placket and the back neck gathers are neatly tucked inside the bindings.

6 With right sides facing, stitch the front and back dress panels together at the side seams. Press the seams open. To create the shoulder ties, pin and baste (tack) a 23$\frac{1}{2}$-in. (60-cm) length of bias binding around the armhole edge and sew it in place. Repeat for the other armhole.

7 To make the hem flounce, with right sides facing, sew together the short ends of the two long fabric strips. Press the seams open. Pin and baste (tack) a 63$\frac{3}{4}$-in. (162-cm) length of bias binding to one long edge and stitch the binding in place along its entire length.

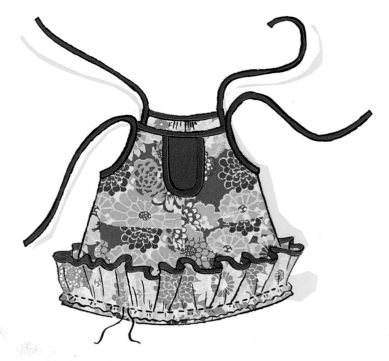

8 Gather the flounce strip so it is the same width as the bottom of the dress. With right sides together, attach the gathered strip to the bottom edge of the dress, ensuring that the gathers are evenly distributed all the way around. Baste (tack) in place and then machine stitch. Sew the buttons to the placket to finish.

Gone Fishin'

A vibrant, sunshine-yellow cotton and a rainbow-colored fish print combine for this smart little beach set. The eyelets at the front are threaded with piping cord to give a truly seaside feel. If you are short of time, replace them with lengths of tape sewn to the edges of the neck slit. The cute coordinated boxer shorts have mock drawstring ties and sporty stripes that run down the outside leg.

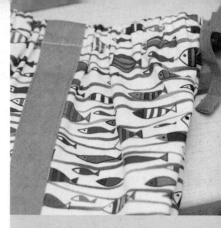

To make the t-shirt

1 Using the pattern pieces provided, cut one front and one back in plain fabric. Cut one front facing, one back neck facing, and two sleeves in print fabric. With right sides facing, machine stitch the front and back panels together at the shoulder seams and press open.

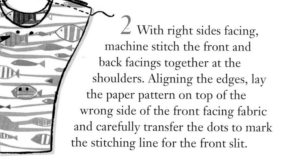

2 With right sides facing, machine stitch the front and back facings together at the shoulders. Aligning the edges, lay the paper pattern on top of the wrong side of the front facing fabric and carefully transfer the dots to mark the stitching line for the front slit.

3 With right sides facing, matching the shoulder seams and aligning all edges, pin the facing to the front and back neck edges. Machine stitch along the seamline at the neck edge and—pivoting with the machine needle—join the dots at the center front. To reinforce the points, stitch over the first stitches.

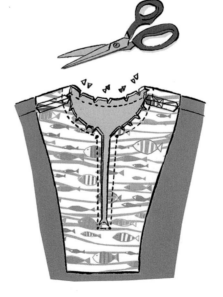

4 Carefully cut the front slit and snip into the corners, avoiding cutting through the machine stitches. Clip the curved neck edge, turn the facing to the inside, and press.

You will need

For the t-shirt
- Pattern B: front (B1), back (B2), sleeve (B3), front facing (B5), and back neck facing (B6)
- Pocket template 2
- 15-in. (38-cm) piece of 35½-in. (90-cm) wide plain fabric
- 9½-in. (24-cm) piece of 35½-in. (90-cm) wide print fabric
- 8 in. (20 cm) bias binding, ¾ in. (20 mm) wide
- 40 in. (100 cm) piping cord, ⅝ in. (15 mm) diameter
- Twelve metal eyelets
- Matching thread

For the beach shorts
- Pattern C: front/back (C1)
- 12 in. (30 cm) piece of 35½-in. (90-cm) wide printed cotton fabric
- 22 in. (56 cm) bias binding, 1 in. (25 mm) wide
- 17¾ in. (45 cm) bias binding in contrast color, 1 in. (25 mm) wide
- 15 in. (38 cm) elastic, ½ in. (12 mm) wide
- Matching thread

Pattern sizes: 3, 6, and 9 months

Note: Take ⅜-in. (1-cm) seam allowances throughout, unless otherwise stated

5 Secure the outer edges of the facing to the front and back panels of the t-shirt with pins and machine stitch through all thicknesses. Mark the positions of the eyelets, punch out holes, and attach the eyelets.

6 To make the little patch pockets, cut two 4-in. (10-cm) squares from the print fabric remnants. Bind the top edges with 4-in. (10-cm) lengths of bias binding (see page 125).

Aligning the top edges, place the pocket template on one of the fabric squares and wrap the excess fabric over it, steam pressing flat as you go around the template. Remove the template and trim down the excess fabric to ³/₈ in. (1 cm). Repeat for the other pocket.

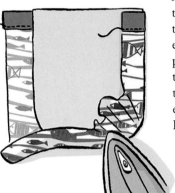

7 Attach the pockets to the front of the t-shirt as illustrated, topstitching close to the side and lower edges of the pockets.

8 To attach the sleeve, stay stitch the armhole ¹/₃ in. (7 mm) in from the cut edge and snip the seam allowance to facilitate easing. With right sides facing, pin the sleeve around the curve of the armhole and machine stitch together. Press open the seam. Repeat for the remaining sleeve. With right sides facing, fold the front panel over onto the back panel. Aligning the cut edges and matching the armhole seams, machine stitch the underarm and side seams as illustrated. Press open the seams.

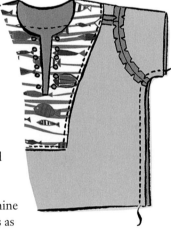

9 On each sleeve and along the bottom of the t-shirt, turn the edges under to the wrong side by ¹/₄ in. (5 mm) and again by ³/₈ in. (1 cm). Pin, baste (tack), and machine stitch as close as possible to the folded edges. Thread the piping cord through the eyelets and tie in a bow. Knot the ends to prevent them from fraying.

To make the beach shorts

1 Using the pattern provided, cut two front/back sections in printed cotton fabric. Before removing the paper pattern, snip into the seam allowances at the balance marks at the center back and top and bottom edges of the shorts. Un-pin the paper pattern.

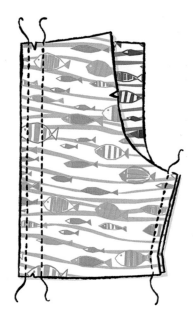

2 Cut two 11-in. (28-cm) lengths of ready-made bias binding. Snip the center points at both ends of each strip. Matching the notches in the binding with the notches in the top and bottom edges of the shorts, lay the strips of binding down the center of the shorts. Edge stitch the strips in place.

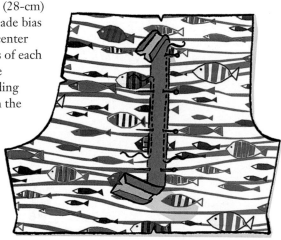

3 With right sides facing and aligning the raw edges, fold one shorts section in half. Pin, baste (tack), and machine stitch the inner leg seam. Repeat for the other leg. Press open the seams.

4 Turn one leg right side out and pull it into the other leg, so that the right sides are facing. With raw edges aligned, pin, baste (tack), and machine stitch along the entire curved center seam from the front top edge to the back top edge. Trim the seam allowance and snip the curves.

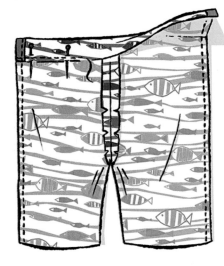

5 To make the casing for the elastic waistband, double hem the top edge by folding over ¼ in. (5 mm) and then ³/₄ in. (2 cm), and press. Pin, baste (tack), and edge stitch the casing in place, leaving a gap in the stitching to insert elastic. Thread elastic through the casing, adjusting it to fit the waist comfortably. Sew the ends together and stitch the opening closed.

6 To make the fake drawstring, fold over the short ends of the bias binding and press. Fold the binding in half along its length, press, and machine stitch along the entire length to secure the fold. Machine stitch the middle of the binding to the top center front waist through all thicknesses and tie it in a neat bow.

7 On each leg of the shorts, turn the bottom edge under to the wrong side by ¹/₄ in. (5 mm) and again by ³/₈ in. (1 cm). Pin, baste (tack), and machine stitch as close as possible to the folded edge.

Gone Fishin'

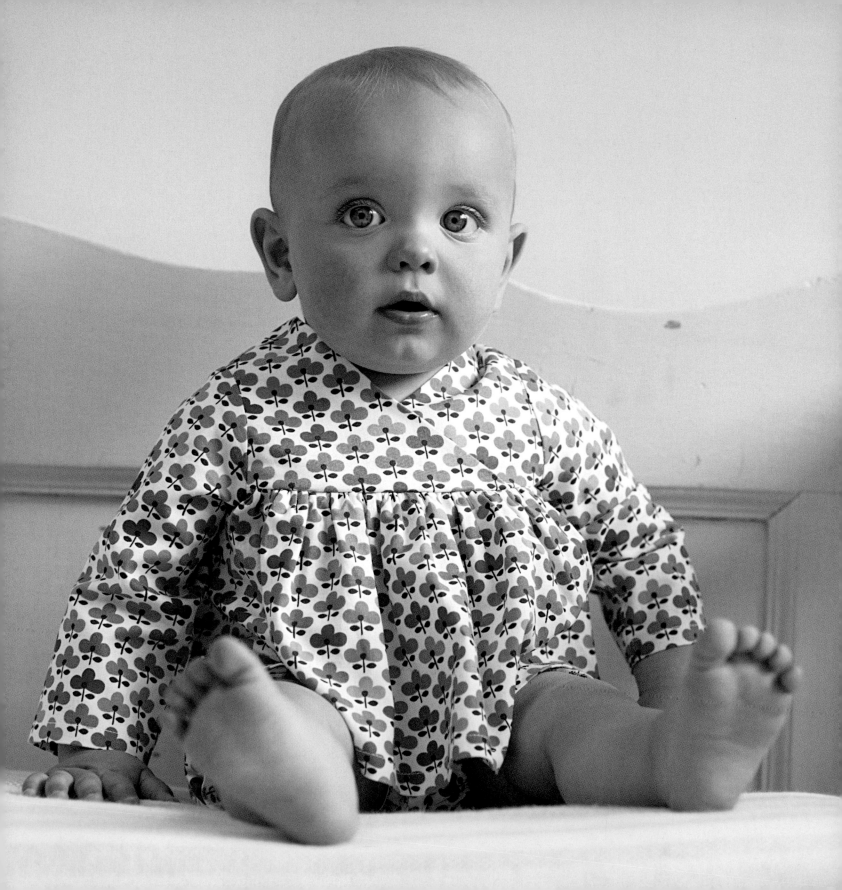

Hello Petal!

This sweet little top is so simple and easy to make—the charming crossover bodice sections use only one pattern piece and the only time-consuming element to this project involves gathering the flounces that create such an adorable silhouette. The lower edges of the pantie legs are elasticated to create pretty ruffled edges, which in turn soften the streamlined geometry of the top.

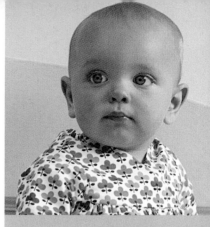

To make the crossover top

1 Remembering to transfer the dot and center front balance mark, trace pattern pieces D1 (x 4), D2, and D3 from the pull-out sheets provided. On double layer fabric, cut out eight bodice pieces and two sleeves.

2 Ensuring that the vertical straight edge of the flounce pattern is aligned and pinned to the folded edge of the fabric, cut out two flounce pieces on the fold. Remember to snip the top edge of the flounce pieces at the center front/back (fold line) as a matching guide.

3 With right sides facing, stitch the eight bodice sections together in pairs at the shoulder seams to create four bodice pieces. Press open the seams. With right sides facing, stitch two bodice pieces together along the curved neckline edge to make the left bodice section. Cut out small notches in the curved seam allowance, turn right side out, and press. Repeat with the remaining pieces to make the right bodice section.

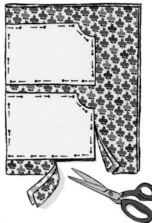

4 Aligning the raw edges and matching the center front balance marks, lay the right bodice on top of the left bodice. Hold the bodice pieces in place with machine stitches, sewing between the dots and $1/3$ in. (7 mm) in from the raw edge.

You will need

For the crossover top

◆ Pattern D: front & back bodice (D1), front & back flounce (D2), and sleeve (D3)
◆ $27\frac{1}{2}$-in. (70-cm) piece of $35\frac{1}{2}$-in. (90-cm) wide print fabric
◆ Matching thread

For the panties

◆ Pattern C: front/back shorts (C1)
◆ 10-in. (25-cm) piece of $35\frac{1}{2}$-in. (90-cm) wide print fabric
◆ $31\frac{1}{2}$ in. (80 cm) elastic, $1/4$ in. (5 mm) wide
◆ Matching thread

Pattern sizes: 3, 6, and 9 months

Note: Take $3/8$-in. (1-cm) seam allowances throughout, unless otherwise stated

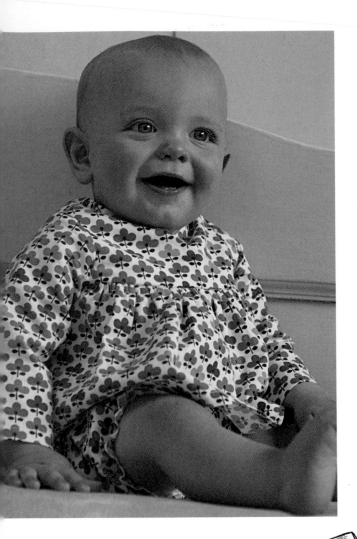

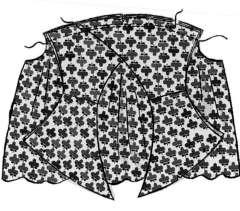

5 Gather the top edge of one flounce by hand or by machine (see page 122), so that it is the same width as the bottom edge of the bodice. With right sides together, pin the flounce to the bottom edge of the front bodice, matching the center front notches and ensuring that the gathers are evenly placed. Baste (tack) and machine stitch. Repeat Steps 4 and 5 to make the back of the crossover top.

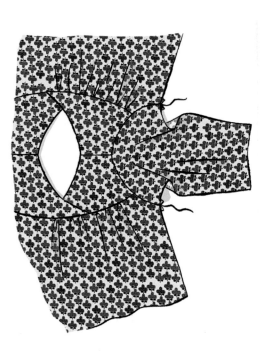

6 To attach the sleeve, stay stitch the armhole ¹/₃ in. (7 mm) in from the cut edge and snip the seam allowance. With right sides facing, matching the balance marks of the sleeve with the shoulder seam of the bodice and the seams that join the bodice to the flounce, pin the sleeve around the curve of the armhole and machine stitch together. Press open the seam. Repeat for the other sleeve.

7 With right sides facing, fold the front over onto the back. Aligning the cut edges and matching the armhole seams, machine stitch the underarm and side seams. Press open the seams. On each sleeve edge and along the bottom of the top, turn the edges under to the wrong side by ¼ in. (5 mm) and again by ³/₈ in. (1 cm). Pin, baste (tack), and machine stitch as close as possible to the folded edges.

To make the panties

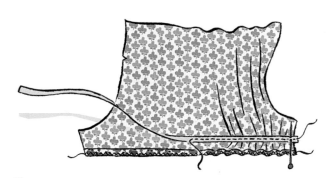

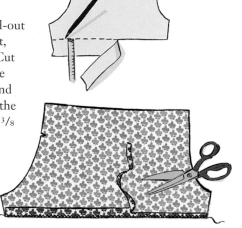

1 Trace pattern C1 from the pull-out sheets provided. Before cutting out, shorten the piece by 2 in. (5 cm). Cut out the new pattern piece along the re-drawn line. Cut out one front and one back from print fabric. Finish the bottom of the legs by folding over 3/8 in. (1 cm), pressing, and finishing with picot edging (see page 125).

2 To ruffle the hem of the panties, cut an 8-in. (20-cm) length of elastic and pin one end to the wrong side of one inside leg edge and the other end to the other edge, approximately 5/8 in. (1.5 cm) in from the picot edge. Place one panties section under your sewing machine, inserting the needle into the elastic and fabric at one end. Sew a few machine stitches to hold the elastic in place. Holding one end of the panties securely with one hand and pulling the other end of the panties with the other hand, stretch the elastic to the width of the hem and carefully stitch through all thicknesses, keeping the fabric lying as flat as possible. Repeat for the other leg section.

3 With right sides facing and aligning the raw edges, fold one panties leg section in half. Pin, baste (tack), and machine stitch the inner leg seam. Repeat for the other leg. Press open the seams.

4 Turn one leg right side out and pull it into the other leg, so that the right sides are facing. With raw edges aligned, pin, baste (tack), and machine stitch along the entire curved center seam from the front top edge to the back top edge. Trim the seam allowance and snip the curves.

5 To make the casing for the elastic waistband, double hem the top edge by folding over 1/4 in. (5 mm) and then 3/4 in. (2 cm), and press. Pin, baste (tack), and edge stitch the casing in place, leaving a gap in the stitching to insert elastic. Thread a 15 3/4-in. (40-cm) length of elastic through the casing, adjusting it to fit the waist comfortably. Sew the ends together and stitch the opening closed.

Hello Petal!

3–6 MONTHS

Chiquita Charm
Bow Belles
Little Linesman

Chiquita Charm

This '60s classic with circular shoulder yoke and gently gathered bodice is festooned with festive pompoms to bring out the "muñeca" in every little girl and is perfect for a piñata party. Multiple bands of rickrack and bias binding add additional zest to the mouth-watering mix of fruit cocktail colors.

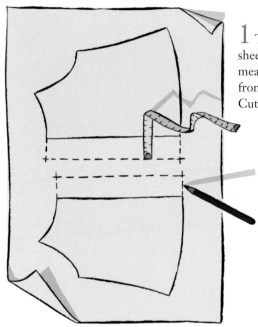

1 Trace pattern pieces A1 and A3 from the pull-out sheets provided. Before cutting out, widen both panels by measuring 1¹/₂ in. (4 cm) out from the straight center front and center back edges, and re-draw the center lines. Cut out the new pattern pieces along the re-drawn lines.

2 Using the new pattern pieces together with the existing ones, cut one front, two front shoulder yokes, two backs, and four back shoulder yokes in plain fabric. Cut two 3 x 35¹/₂-in. (8 x 90-cm) lengths of fabric for the hem flounce. With right sides together, stitch the two back sections to the dress front at the side seams. Press open.

3 Pin and baste (tack) a 10-in. (25-cm) length of bias binding around the armhole and edge stitch the binding in place (see page 125). Pin, baste, and machine stitch a 13-in. (33-cm) length of rickrack below the armhole binding as illustrated. Repeat for the other armhole. Lay the dress right side up on your work surface. Pin, baste, and machine stitch the 37¹/₂-in. (95-cm) lengths of rickrack and pompom trim across the entire width of the dress.

You will need

- Pattern A: front (A1), front shoulder yoke (A2), back (A3), and back shoulder yoke (A4)
- 24¹/₂-in. (62-cm) piece of 45-in. (112-cm) wide plain fabric
- 70³/₄ in. (180 cm) pink bias binding, 1 in. (25 mm) wide
- 10 in. (25 cm) turquoise bias binding, 1 in. (25 mm) wide
- 10 in. (25 cm) lime green bias binding, 1 in. (25 mm) wide
- 37¹/₂ in. (95 cm) each of turquoise and lime green pompom trim
- 13 in. (33 cm) each of pink and yellow jumbo rickrack
- 37¹/₂ in. (95 cm) each of red and lilac jumbo rickrack
- 7 in. (18 cm) zipper fastener
- Matching thread

Pattern sizes: 3, **6**, and 9 months

Note: Take ³/₈-in. (1-cm) seam allowances throughout, unless otherwise stated

4 With right sides together, stitch the outer front shoulder yoke to the outer back shoulder yokes at the shoulder seams and press open the seams. Gather the top edges of the front and back dress by hand or by machine (see page 122).

5 With right sides together, pin the outer yoke to the front and back panels of the dress, matching up the outer edges of the armholes with the reference dots on the yoke. Adjusting the gathers to fit the outer yoke, pin, baste (tack), and machine stitch in place.

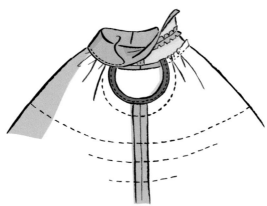

6 With right sides together, stitch the inner front shoulder yoke to the inner back shoulder yokes at the shoulder seams and press open the seams. As a folding guide, machine stitch around the entire inner yoke ³/₈ in. (1 cm) from the raw edge. Carefully fold to the wrong side and press.

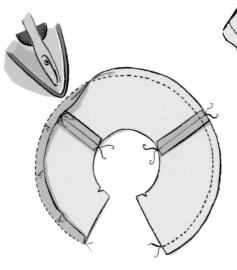

7 With right sides together and matching the shoulder seams, pin and baste (tack) the outer yoke to the inner yoke at the neck edge. Machine stitch together and snip the curved edges.

8 Turn the dress inside out. Turn the inner yoke over to the inside of the dress and carefully match up the edges of both yokes, especially at the armholes. Ensuring that the yokes are lying flat, the shoulder seams match up, and the ends of the bound armholes are neatly tucked inside, pin, baste (tack), and carefully edge stitch the entire yoke.

3–6 Months

9 With right sides facing, machine stitch the back panels together at the center back seam approximately 7 in. (18 cm) in from the bottom edge. Make several backstitches to reinforce the seam. Press open the seam and the remaining seam allowances that will form the back opening.

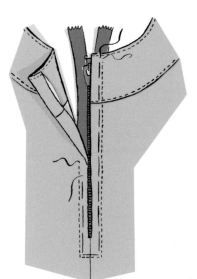

10 With pressed center back edges meeting, place the zipper fastener underneath the dress and carefully baste (tack) in place. Following the basting stitches, machine stitch the zipper to the dress through all thicknesses. Fold over the ends of the zipper to finish.

11 With right sides facing, pin and machine stitch together the short edges of the two long strips of fabric that form the hem flounce. Press the seams open. Pin and baste (tack) the 70¾-in. (180-cm) length of bias binding to one edge and stitch the binding in place along its entire length (see page 125). Gather the strip so that it is the same width as the bottom of the dress (see page 122). With right sides together, attach the gathered strip to the bottom edge of the dress, ensuring that the gathers are even all the way around. Baste (tack) in place and then machine stitch.

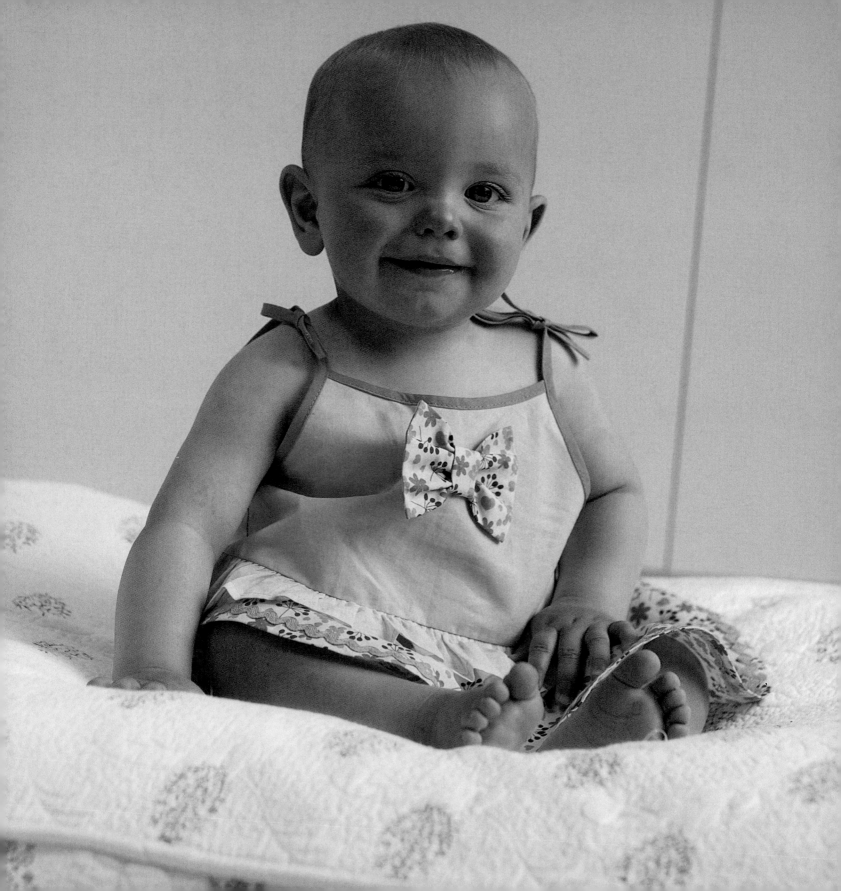

Bow Belles

Fine, contrast bindings are a pretty and practical feature of this featherweight camisole top. Delicately encircling the neck and arms, they form the sweetest— and easiest-to-make—bow ties at the shoulder. A cheesecloth (muslin) hem flounce adds to the overall sense of lightness, while an oversized pussycat bow increases the fun factor. Rickrack trim provides the finishing touch to the charming little circle skirt featured in a coordinating floral print.

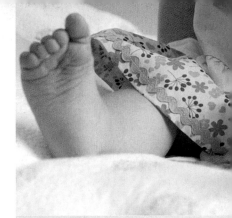

To make the camisole

1 Trace pattern pieces A1 and A3. Before cutting out, shorten the front and back panels by 5½ in. (14 cm). Cut out the new pattern pieces along the re-drawn lines. Using the new pattern pieces, cut one front and one back in the folded plain fabric, and cut two 3 x 23-in. (7.5 x 58-cm) strips in cheesecloth (muslin).

2 Following the instructions on page 122, gather 2¼ in. (6 cm) of the center back neck by hand or by machine to 1¼ in. (3 cm), approximately ¼ in. (5 mm) in from the raw edge. Press the gathers flat.

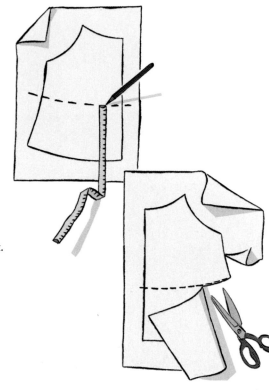

3 Carefully bind the front and back neck edges with 7-in. (18-cm) lengths of bias binding. With right sides together, stitch the back panel to the front panel at the side seams and press open. Pin and baste (tack) a 25½-in. (65-cm) length of bias binding around the armhole and edge stitch the binding in place (see page 125). Repeat for the other armhole.

4 To make the hem flounce, with right sides facing, pin and machine stitch together the two lengths of cheesecloth (muslin) to form a loop. Press open the seams. Double hem the loop, turning the bottom edge over to the wrong side by ¼ in. (5 mm) and again by ⅜ in. (1 cm). Pin, baste (tack), and machine stitch as close as possible to the folded edge.

(see page 122)

You will need

For the camisole
- Pattern A: front (A1) and back (A3)
- 8-in. (20-cm) piece of 45-in. (112-cm) wide plain fabric
- 7 x 8-in. (18 x 20-cm) piece of printed fabric for the "pussycat" bow
- 6 x 23-in. (15 x 58-cm) piece of plain cheesecloth (muslin) to match plain fabric
- 65¼ in. (166 cm) bias binding, ½ in. (12 mm) wide
- Matching thread

For the circle skirt
- Pattern E: front/back (E1)
- 15¾-in. (40-cm) piece of 45-in. (112-cm) wide print fabric
- 59 in. (150 cm) pink rickrack trim
- 17¼ in. (44 cm) elastic, ½ in. (12 mm) wide
- Matching thread

Pattern sizes: 3, **6**, and 9 months

Note: Take ⅜-in. (1-cm) seam allowances throughout, unless otherwise stated

Bow Belles

5 Gather the loop into a flounce, so that it is the same width as the bottom of the camisole (see page 122). With right sides facing, pin the flounce to the bottom edge of the camisole, ensuring that the gathers are evenly placed all the way around. Baste (tack) and then machine stitch.

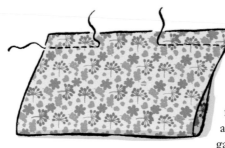

6 To make the bow, cut a 2$\frac{1}{4}$ x 3-in. (6 x 8-cm) rectangle for the "knot" and a 4$\frac{3}{4}$ x 6$\frac{1}{4}$-in. (12 x 16-cm) rectangle for the "bow" in print fabric. With right sides together, fold the large rectangle of fabric in half at the shorter ends and machine stitch along the raw edge (opposite the folded edge), leaving a gap in the seam.

7 Re-fold the rectangle so that the seam is in the center and gently press the seam allowances to either side. Machine stitch closed the opening at each side, snip off the corners, turn right side out through the opening, and gently press.

8 Sew the opening closed with hand stitches, gather the bow in the center, secure with a few hand stitches, and put to one side.

9 To make the "knot," with right sides together, fold the small rectangle of fabric in half at the longer ends and machine stitch along the raw edge (opposite the folded edge). Turn right side out, re-fold the rectangle so that the seam is in the center, and gently press.

10 Wrap the "knot" around the "bow" to cover the gathers and secure at the back with hand stitches. Hand stitch the bow to the front of the camisole.

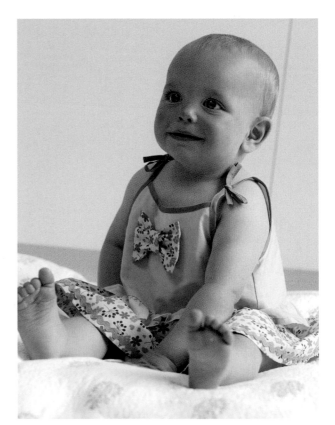

3–6 Months

To make the circle skirt

1 Using the pattern provided, cut two front/back sections and a 2¾ x 21-in. (7 x 53-cm) strip for the waistband in printed cotton fabric. Before removing the paper pattern, snip into the center fold line at the top edges of the skirt panels. Fold the waistband "strip" in half lengthwise and snip into the center fold line.

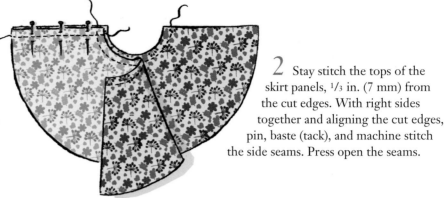

2 Stay stitch the tops of the skirt panels, ⅓ in. (7 mm) from the cut edges. With right sides together and aligning the cut edges, pin, baste (tack), and machine stitch the side seams. Press open the seams.

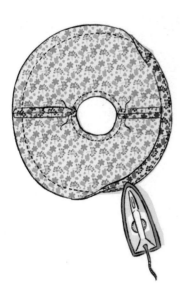

3 Using the longest stitch length, machine stitch ⅝ in. (1.5 cm) in from the bottom edge. Using the stitching line as a guide, fold under the seam allowance on the stitching line, press, and baste (tack) to hold in place. To finish the hem, topstitch through all thicknesses approximately ⅜ in. (1 cm) in from the folded edge. Remove the basting and guideline stitches. Conceal the topstitching by sewing a length of rickrack along the edge of the skirt.

4 Fold the waistband in half lengthwise and press in a crease. Open out the folded waistband. Along the entire length of one long edge, fold over ⅜ in. (1 cm) and press. With right sides facing, machine stitch together the short ends as illustrated, and press open the seam.

5 Pin the waistband to the skirt. Carefully snipping into the seam allowance along the curved top edge of the skirt panels will make it easier to attach to the straight edge of the waistband. Matching the notches at the center front of the waistband and skirt, machine stitch together.

6 Trim down the seam allowances, fold the waistband over to the inside, and edge stitch in place, stitching as close as possible to the folded edge and leaving a gap in the stitching to insert elastic. Thread elastic through the waistband casing, adjusting it to fit the waist comfortably. Sew the ends together and stitch the opening closed.

Bow Belles

Little Linesman

Little men and tomboys will stay comfortable all day long in this miniature version of a "workwear" classic. Designed with simplicity in mind, this jaunty playsuit features a minimum of seams to avoid uncomfortable bulk. Cut in bold, vintage-look cotton awning stripe, this kidswear favorite is accented with "jean-style" double topstitching, high-visibility pocket bindings, and jolly, lollipop-bright press-stud closures.

You will need:

- Pattern F: front pant (F1), front facing (F2), front waistband (F3), front/back bib (F4), back pant (F5), side extension (F6), back waistband (F7), and shoulder strap (F8)
- Pocket templates 1, 3, and 4
- 30-in. (75-cm) piece of 54-in. (138-cm) wide striped fabric
- 15 in. (38 cm) purple bias binding, 1 in. (25 mm) wide
- 3½ in. (9 cm) yellow bias binding, 1 in. (25 mm) wide
- Six x ½ in. (12 mm) press-stud fasteners in assorted colors
- Matching thread

Pattern sizes: 3, **6**, and 9 months

Note: Take ³/₈-in. (1-cm) seam allowances throughout, unless otherwise stated

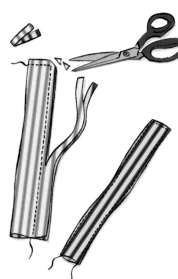

1 Trace the pattern from the pull-out sheets provided, remembering to transfer all balance marks. Cut two front pants, two front facings, two front waistbands, four front/back bibs, two back pants, two side extensions, two back waistbands, and two shoulder straps.

2 With right sides facing, fold a shoulder strap in half lengthwise and machine stitch together, leaving one short end open. Trim off ¹/₄ in. (5 mm) from the seam allowance and trim the corners diagonally. Turn the strap right side out, press, and double topstitch close to the edge. Repeat for the second strap.

3 To make the patch pockets for the back pants, cut two 4³/₄-in. (12-cm) squares from the fabric remnants (if using striped fabric, position the stripes horizontally for contrast). Bind the top edge of one square with a 4³/₄-in. (12-cm) length of purple bias binding (see page 125). Aligning the top edges, place template 3 on the fabric square and wrap the excess fabric over it, steam pressing flat as you go around the template. Remove the template and trim down the excess fabric to ³/₈ in. (1 cm). Repeat for the second pocket.

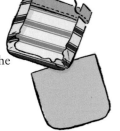

4 To make the "coin" pocket for the front pants, cut one 3¹/₂-in. (9-cm) square from the fabric remnants. Bind the top edge of the square with a 3¹/₂-in. (9-cm) length of yellow bias binding. Using template 1, make as for the back patch pockets. To make the patch pocket for the front bib, cut a 3 x 5¹/₂-in. (8 x 14-cm) rectangle from the fabric remnants. Bind the top edge with a 5¹/₂-in. (14-cm) length of purple bias binding. Using template 4, make as above.

5 Pin and baste (tack) the bib pocket to a bib piece approximately 1¹/₄ in. (3.5 cm) down from the upper edge of the bib. Topstitch close to the side and lower edges of the pocket. Sew a line of machine stitches down the center of the pocket to create two pouches. With right sides together and aligning the raw edges, lay one bib piece on top of the bib piece with the pocket attached. Pin, baste (tack), and machine stitch all the way around apart from the straight lower edge. Trim the seam allowance and clip the corners. Turn right side out, press, and close the opening with a row of stay stitches. Double topstitch the bib close to the edges.

6 To assemble the back bib, pin the shoulder straps to a bib piece ³/₈ in. (1 cm) in from the top side of the bib, and secure with machine stitches. With right sides together and aligning the raw edges, lay the remaining bib piece on top of the bib piece with straps attached. Pin, baste (tack), and machine stitch all the way around apart from the straight lower edge. Turn right side out, press, and close the opening with a row of stay stitches. Double topstitch the bib close to the edges.

7 Attach the coin pocket to the left front leg approximately 4 in. (10 cm) down from the upper edge of the front leg. Topstitch close to the side and lower edges of the pocket. With right sides facing, stitch the front pant pieces together at the center seam. Press open the seam, turn the front pant section right side up, and topstitch a fake fly front on the left pant piece, as illustrated. Stitch two bars of close zigzag stitching to create a more realistic effect.

3–6 Months

8 With right sides together, stitch the front facings to the right side of the front pant pieces along the top side edges. Turn the front facings to the inside, press, and double topstitch close to the edges.

9 With right sides facing and matching the center front notches, stitch one front waistband to the upper edge of the front pants. With right sides facing and matching the center front notches, stitch the bib without shoulder straps to the upper edge of the front waistband.

Little Linesman

10 Press the seam allowance at the lower edge of the other front waistband to the wrong side and trim off the overlap. With right sides facing, stitch the two front waistband pieces together along the upper and side edges, as illustrated, ensuring that the bib is caught in between.

11 Trim 1/4 in. (5 mm) from the seam allowance along the upper and side edges of the front waistband, and trim the corners diagonally. Turn the waistband right side out and press. Slipstitch the opening closed, ensuring that the seam allowance is neatly tucked inside and out of view. Turn the front section of the dungarees over to the right side and topstitch the front waistband close to the edges.

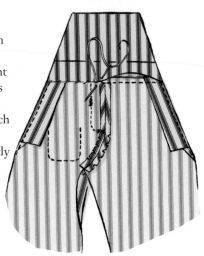

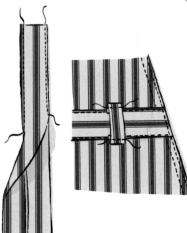

12 To make belt loops, cut a 2 1/4 x 6 1/4-in. (6 x 16-cm) strip from the fabric remnants. Press the long edges of the strip to the center and then press the strip in half lengthwise. Topstitch close to both folded edges. Cut the strip into two equal lengths and turn the ends under. Pin the belt loops to the front waistband and machine stitch the upper and lower edges through all thicknesses.

13 To make the back section of the dungarees, attach a patch pocket to each of the back pants legs approximately 2 1/4 in. (6 cm) down from the upper edge. Topstitch close to the side and lower edges of the pockets. Stitch the back pant sections together at the center seam and press open.

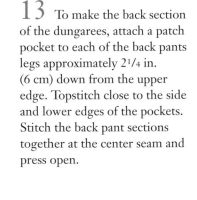

14 With wrong sides facing, fold the side extension pieces in half and press. With right sides together, stitch them to the back pant pieces, as illustrated. Press the side extensions and seam allowance away from the center of the pants.

15 With right sides facing and matching the center back notches, stitch one back waistband to the upper edge of the back pants. Attach the back bib and complete the back waistband in the same way as the front (see Steps 9 and 10).

3–6 Months

16 Lay the front dungarees section on the back dungarees section, right sides together, and machine stitch together along the side seams. Start stitching at the point where the edge of the front facing and the side extension seam converge. Press the seam allowance.

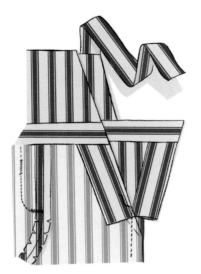

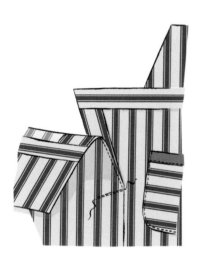

17 Stitch a double row of stitches on the front pants section below the opening, as illustrated, to hold the side extension in place. Repeat for the other side. On each leg of the pants, turn the bottom edge to the wrong side by 1/4 in. (5 mm) and again by 3/8 in. (1 cm). Pin, baste (tack), and machine stitch as close as possible to the folded edge.

18 Lay the front pants on the back pants, with right sides together. Pin, baste (tack), and machine stitch along the inside leg seams, matching the center front and center back seams. Snip the curved edges and press the seam open.

19 Following the manufacturer's instructions, attach press-stud fasteners to each end of the front and back waistbands, at the mid-point along the side openings and the side extensions. Determine the correct fit before attaching press-studs to the ends of the shoulder straps and the upper edge of the front bib. Attaching additional bottom halves of press-stud fasteners to the shoulder straps will provide adjustability.

Little Linesman

6–9 MONTHS

Animal Magic
Washday Blues
Butterfly Fun
Garden Miniature

Animal Magic

This funky print of exotic wildlife enlivens a simple circle skirt. Tessa the tiger, Elsa the elephant, and Zack the zebra have been taken from the printed fabric to create charming appliqués that wander freely across the bodice of the little top. Look out for similar nursery prints or florals that are suitable motifs to cut out and use as eye-catching embellishment.

To make the sun top

1 Trace pattern pieces A1 and A3. Before cutting out, shorten the front and back panels by 4 in. (10 cm). Cut out the new pattern pieces along the re-drawn lines. Using the new pattern pieces together with the existing ones, cut one front and two backs in plain fabric. Cut two front shoulder yokes and four back shoulder yokes in print fabric.

2 With right sides together, stitch the two back panels to the front panel at the side seams and press open. Pin and baste (tack) an 11-in. (28-cm) length of orange bias binding around the armhole and edge stitch in place (see page 125). Repeat for the other armhole.

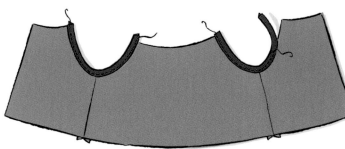

3 To make the appliqués, take the remnants of print fabric, and following the manufacturer's instructions, back them with fusible bonding web. Carefully cut out the motifs. Lay the dress right side up on your work surface. Position the appliqués on the top in a pleasing arrangement. Apply to the front and back (see page 125).

You will need
For the sun top
- Pattern A: front (A1), front shoulder yoke (A2), back (A3), and back shoulder yoke (A4)
- 12-in. (30-cm) piece of 35½-in. (90-cm) wide plain fabric
- 10¼-in. (26-cm) piece of 35½-in. (90-cm) wide print fabric
- 30¾ in. (78 cm) blue bias binding, ½ in. (12 mm) wide
- 22 in. (56 cm) orange bias binding, ½ in. (12 mm) wide
- Fusible bonding web
- 6-in. (15-cm) zipper fastener
- Matching thread

For the circle skirt
- Pattern E: front/back (E1)
- 27½-in. (70-cm) piece of 35½-in. (90-cm) wide print fabric
- 66 in. (168 cm) pale blue bias binding, ½ in. (12 mm) wide
- 18 in. (46 cm) elastic, ½ in. (12 mm) wide
- Matching thread

Pattern sizes: 3, 6, and **9** months

Note: Take ³/₈-in. (1-cm) seam allowances throughout, unless otherwise stated

4 With right sides facing, machine stitch the outer front and back shoulder yokes together, and the inner front and back shoulder yokes together at the shoulder seams, and press open the seams. As a folding guide, machine stitch ³/₈ in. (1 cm) in from the outer cut edges of the yokes.

5 With right sides together, pin the outer yoke to the front and back panels of the sun top, matching up the outer edges of the armholes with the reference dots on the yoke. Baste (tack) and machine stitch in place.

6 Following the stitching line guide, carefully fold under the seam allowance of the inner yoke and press.

7 With right sides together and matching the shoulder seams, pin and baste (tack) the outer yoke to the inner yoke at the neck edge. Machine stitch together and cut out wedges in the curved seam allowance.

8 Turn the inner yoke over to the inside and carefully match up the edges of both yokes, especially at the armholes. Ensuring that the yokes are lying flat, the shoulder seams match up, and the ends of the bound armholes are neatly tucked inside, pin, baste (tack), and carefully edge stitch the entire yoke.

9 With right sides facing, machine stitch the back panels together at the center back seam approximately 5 in. (13 cm) in from the bottom edge. Make several backstitches to reinforce the seam. Press open the seam and the remaining seam allowances that will form the center back opening. Place the zipper fastener underneath the center back opening and carefully baste (tack) in place. Following the basting stitches, machine stitch the zipper fastener to the garment through all thicknesses.

10 Pin and baste (tack) a 30¾-in. (78-cm) length of blue bias binding along the entire hem and edge stitch the binding in place (see page 125).

To make the circle skirt

1 Using the pattern provided, cut two front/back sections and a 2¾ x 22-in. (7 x 56-cm) strip for the waistband in printed cotton fabric. Before removing the paper pattern, snip into the center fold line at the top edges of the skirt panels. Un-pin the paper pattern. Fold the waistband "strip" in half lengthwise and snip into the center fold line.

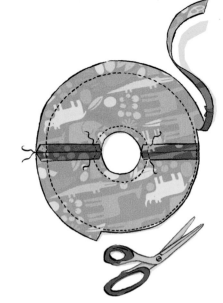

2 Stay stitch the tops of the skirt panels, ⅓ in. (7 mm) from the cut edges. With right sides together and aligning the cut edges, pin, baste (tack), and machine stitch the side seams. Press open the seams. Machine stitch ⅝ in. (1.5 cm) in from the bottom edge and trim off the seam allowance, cutting as close as possible to the stitching line. Bind the hem with the long length of bias binding.

3 Fold the waistband in half lengthwise and press in a crease. Open out the waistband. Along the entire length of one long edge, fold over ⅜ in. (1 cm) and press. With right sides facing, machine stitch together the short ends and press open the seam.

4 Pin the waistband to the skirt. Carefully snipping into the seam allowance along the curved top edge of the skirt panels will make it easier to attach to the straight edge of the waistband. Matching the notches at the center front of the waistband and skirt, machine stitch together.

5 Trim down the seam allowances, fold the waistband over to the inside, and edge stitch in place, stitching as close as possible to the folded edge and leaving a gap in the stitching to insert elastic. Thread the elastic through the waistband casing, adjusting it to fit the waist comfortably. Sew the ends together and stitch the opening closed.

Washday Blues

Laundered ticking stripes and French country florals in faded cornflower blue are mixed and matched to suggest an air of relaxed, bohemian charm. This little boy's hippie tunic and pajama pants—great for lounging around at home—are packed full of great detailing. The top features a contrasting back panel, while the pants have four roomy patch pockets with button trim and a mini-pocket with a cute little binding.

To make the lace-up top

1 Using the pattern pieces provided, cut one front and two sleeves in striped fabric. Cut one back, one front facing, and one back neck facing in floral fabric. With right sides facing, machine stitch the front and back shirt panels together at the shoulder seams and press open.

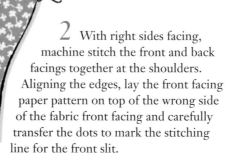

2 With right sides facing, machine stitch the front and back facings together at the shoulders. Aligning the edges, lay the front facing paper pattern on top of the wrong side of the fabric front facing and carefully transfer the dots to mark the stitching line for the front slit.

3 With right sides facing, matching the shoulder seams and aligning all edges, pin the facing to the front and back neck edge. Machine stitch along the seamline at the neck edge and—pivoting with the machine needle—join the dots at the center front. To reinforce the points, stitch over the first stitching.

4 Carefully cut the front slit and snip into the corners, avoiding cutting through the machine stitches. Clip the curved neck edge, turn the facing to the inside, and press.

You will need

For the lace-up top

- Pattern B: front (B1), back (B2), sleeve (B4), front facing (B5), and back neck facing (B6)
- 15-in. (38-cm) piece of 35½-in. (90-cm) wide striped fabric
- 8-in. (20-cm) piece of 35½-in. (90-cm) wide floral fabric
- 40 in. (100 cm) piping cord, ⅝ in. (15 mm) diameter
- Twelve metal eyelets
- Matching thread

For the 5-pocket pants

- Pattern G: front/back (G1)
- Pocket pattern 3
- Pocket template 2
- 25½-in. (65-cm) piece of 35½-in. (90-cm) wide floral fabric
- 4 in. (10 cm) bias binding in contrast color, 1 in. (25 mm) wide
- 15 in. (38 cm) elastic, ½ in. (12 mm) wide
- Four x ¾ in. (18 mm) diameter buttons
- Matching thread

Pattern sizes: 3, 6, and **9** months

Note: Take ⅜-in. (1-cm) seam allowances throughout, unless otherwise stated

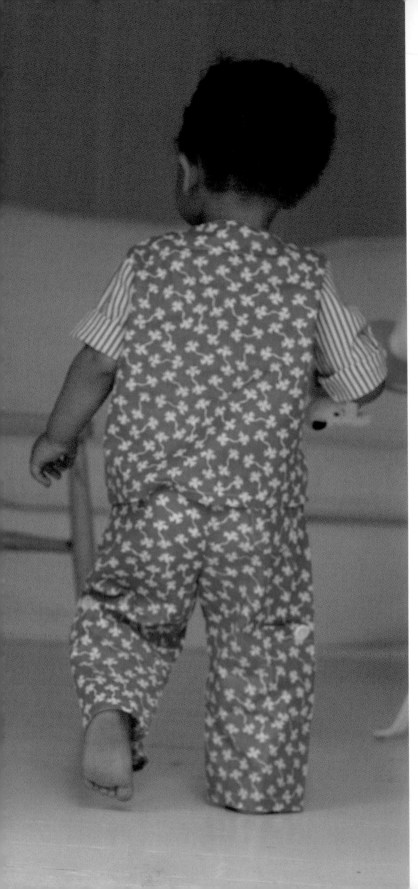

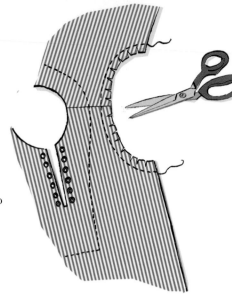

5 Secure the outer edges of the facing to the front and back panels of the t-shirt with pins and machine stitch through all thicknesses. Mark the positions of the eyelets, punch out holes, and attach the eyelets. To attach the sleeve, stay stitch the armhole $1/3$ in. (7 mm) in from the cut edge and snip the allowance to facilitate easing.

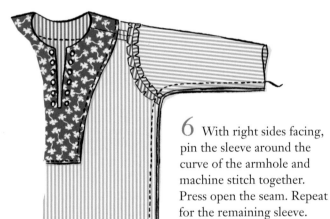

6 With right sides facing, pin the sleeve around the curve of the armhole and machine stitch together. Press open the seam. Repeat for the remaining sleeve. With right sides facing, fold the front panel over onto the back panel. Aligning the cut edges and matching the armhole seams, machine stitch the underarm and side seams as illustrated. Press open the seams.

7 On each sleeve and along the bottom of the t-shirt, turn the edges under to the wrong side by $1/4$ in. (5 mm) and again by $3/8$ in. (1 cm). Pin, baste (tack), and machine stitch as close as possible to the folded edges. Thread the piping cord through the eyelets and tie in a bow. Knot the ends to prevent them from fraying.

To make the 5-pocket pants

1 Using the pattern pieces provided, cut two front/back sections and four pockets in printed cotton fabric. Make the four "contour-stitched" patch pockets (see page 124), and sew buttonholes to the upper areas. Remember to cut open the buttonholes before attaching the pockets to the leg sections.

2 Pin and baste (tack) a pocket to each seat of the pants, with the top edge of the pocket approximately $2^3/4$ in. (7 cm) down from the top raw edge of the pants. Topstitch close to the side and lower edges of the pockets. Place the two side pockets approximately $9^1/2$ in. (24 cm) down from the top raw edge, and toward the front area. Pin, baste, and machine stitch in place.

3 To make the coin pocket, cut a 4-in. (10-cm) square from the fabric remnants. Bind the top edge with a 4-in. (10-cm) length of bias binding (see page 125). Aligning the top edges, place the template on the fabric square and wrap the excess fabric over it, steam pressing flat as you go around the template. Remove the template and trim down the excess fabric to $3/8$ in. (1 cm).

4 Attach the coin pocket to the front of the pants as illustrated, topstitching close to the side and lower edges of the pocket.

5 With right sides facing and aligning the raw edges, fold one pant leg in half. Pin, baste (tack), and machine stitch the inner leg seam together. Repeat for the other leg. Press open the seams. Turn one leg right side out and pull it into the other leg, so that the right sides are facing. With raw edges aligned, pin, baste (tack), and machine stitch along the entire curved center seam from the front top edge to the back top edge. Trim the seam allowance and snip the curves.

6 To make the casing for the elastic waistband, double hem the top edge by folding over $1/4$ in. (5 mm) and then $3/4$ in. (2 cm), and press. Pin, baste (tack), and edge stitch the casing in place, leaving a gap in the stitching to insert elastic. Thread elastic through the casing, adjusting it to fit the waist comfortably. Sew the ends together and stitch the opening closed.

7 On each leg of the pants, turn the bottom edge under to the wrong side by $1/4$ in. (5 mm) and again by $3/8$ in. (1 cm). Pin, baste (tack), and machine stitch as close as possible to the folded edge. Sew a button to the pants underneath the buttonhole of each patch pocket.

Washday Blues

Butterfly Fun

This sweet little blouse is a variation on the boys' tops Gone Fishin' (see page 14) and Washday Blues (see page 44). Here, to create an attractive contrasting neckline, the front facing is turned and attached to the outside, not to the inside. The lower edges of the sleeves and the legs of the panties are elasticated to create delicate ruffled edges. Pretty ribbon ties embellish the front and a larger-than-life butterfly gently hovers at the hemline.

To make the blouse

1 Using the pattern pieces provided, cut one front and one back in plain fabric. Cut one front facing, one back neck facing, and two sleeves in print fabric. With right sides facing, machine stitch together the front and back panels at the shoulder seams and press the seams open.

2 With right sides facing, machine stitch the front and back facings together at the shoulders. Aligning the edges, lay the front facing paper pattern on top of the wrong side of the fabric front facing and carefully transfer the dots to mark the stitching line for the front slit. Using the longest stitch length, machine stitch around the entire facing 3/8 in. (1 cm) in from the edge. Fold under the raw edge along the stitching line, press, and baste (tack) to hold in place.

3 Matching the shoulder seams and aligning all edges, pin the wrong side of the facing to the wrong side of the front and neck edge. Machine stitch along the seamline at the neck edge and—pivoting with the machine needle— join the dots at the center front. To reinforce the points, stitch over the first stitching. Carefully cut the front slit and snip into the corners, avoiding cutting through the machine stitches. Clip the curved neck edge, turn the facing to the outside, and press.

4 Pin the front and back facing to the front and back panels of the tunic, and zigzag stitch on the folded edge through all thicknesses.

You will need

For the blouse

◆ Pattern B: front (B1), back (B2), long sleeve (B4), front neck facing (B5), and back neck facing (B6)
◆ Butterfly Fun appliqué motif
◆ 11-in. (28-cm) piece of 57-in. (145-cm) wide print fabric
◆ 15¾-in. (40-cm) piece of 57-in. (145-cm) wide plain fabric
◆ 40 in. (100 cm) satin ribbon, ¼ in. (5 mm) wide
◆ 9½ in. (24 cm) elastic, ¼ in. (5 mm) wide
◆ Fusible bonding web
◆ Matching thread
◆ Embroidery floss (thread)

For the panties

◆ Pattern C: front/back shorts (C1)
◆ 10-in. (25-cm) piece of 45-in. (112-cm) wide print fabric
◆ 31½ in. (80 cm) elastic, ¼ in. (5 mm) wide
◆ Matching thread

Pattern sizes: 3, **6**, and 9 months

Note: Take 3/8-in. (1-cm) seam allowances throughout, unless otherwise stated

5 To make the butterfly appliqué for the front panel of the tunic, take a scrap of print fabric and, following the manufacturer's instructions, back it with fusible bonding web. Apply the motif (see page 125). Embroider antennae in backstitch.

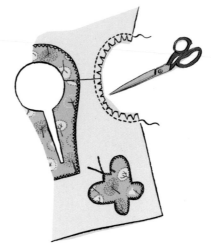

6 To attach the sleeve, stay stitch the armhole ¼ in. (5 mm) in from the cut edge and snip the allowance to facilitate easing. With right sides facing, pin the sleeve around the curve of the armhole and machine stitch together. Press open the seam. Repeat for the remaining sleeve.

7 Finish the bottom of the sleeves by folding over ³/₈ in. (1 cm), pressing, and finishing with picot edging (see page 125). To ruffle the hem of the sleeve, cut a 4¾-in. (12-cm) length of elastic. Pin one end to the wrong side of one underarm edge and the other end to the other underarm edge, approximtely ⁵/₈ in. (1.5 cm) in from the picot edge. Place one sleeve, wrong side up, under your sewing machine, inserting the needle into the elastic and fabric at one end. Sew a few machine stitches to hold the elastic in place. Holding one edge of the sleeve securely with one hand and pulling the other edge of the sleeve with the other hand, stretch the elastic to the width of the sleeve hem and carefully stitch through all thickness, remembering to keep the fabric lying as flat as possible. Repeat for the other sleeve.

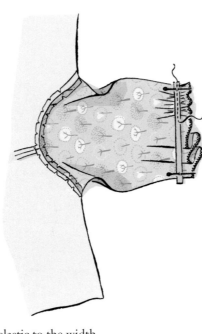

8 With right sides facing, fold the front panel over onto the back panel. Aligning the cut edges and matching the armhole seams, machine stitch the underarm and side seams as illustrated. Press open the seams.

9 Along the bottom of the tunic, turn the edges under to the wrong side by ¼ in. (5 mm) and again by ³/₈ in. (1 cm). Pin, baste (tack), and machine stitch as close as possible to the folded edges. Cut four 10-in. (25-cm) lengths of satin ribbon for the neck ties and attach to the front as illustrated.

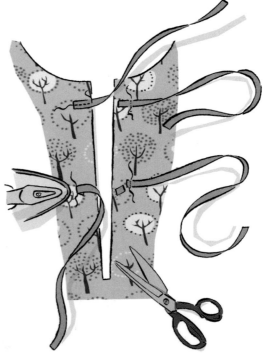

To make the panties

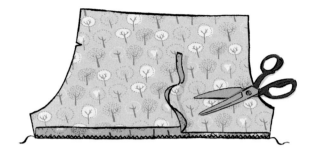

1 Trace pattern C1 from the pull-out sheets provided. Before cutting out, shorten by 2 in. (5 cm). Cut out the new pattern piece along the re-drawn line. Cut one front and one back from print fabric. Finish the bottom of the legs by folding over 3/8 in. (1 cm), pressing, and finishing with picot edging (see page 125).

2 To ruffle the hem of the panties, cut an 8-in. (20-cm) length of elastic. Pin one end to the wrong side of one inside leg edge and the other end to the other edge, approximately 5/8 in. (1.5 cm) in from the picot edge. Place one pants section under your sewing machine, inserting the needle into the elastic and fabric at one end. Sew a few machine stitches to hold the elastic in place. Holding one end of the panties securely with one hand and pulling the other end of the panties with the other hand, stretch the elastic to the width of the hem and carefully stitch through all thicknesses, keeping the fabric lying as flat as possible. Repeat for the other leg.

3 With right sides facing and aligning the raw edges, fold one leg section in half. Pin, baste (tack), and machine stitch the inner leg seam. Repeat for the other leg. Press open the seams.

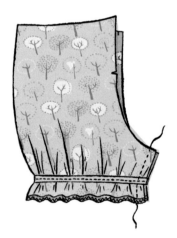

4 Turn one leg right side out and pull it into the other leg, so that the right sides are facing. With raw edges aligned, pin, baste (tack), and machine stitch along the entire curved center seam from the front top edge to the back top edge. Trim the seam allowance and snip the curves.

5 To make the casing for the elastic waistband, double hem the top edge by folding over ¼ in. (5 mm) and then ¾ in. (2 cm) and press. Pin, baste (tack), and edge stitch the casing in place, leaving a gap in the stitching to insert elastic. Thread a 15¾-in. (40-cm) length of elastic through the casing, adjusting it to fit the waist comfortably. Sew the ends together and stitch the opening closed.

Garden Miniature

Minute motifs of fauna and flora add a delicate touch to this hybrid of the classic "workwear" staple—the dungarees. Flaring skirt panels replace traditional pant legs and cute little shoulder ties replace the standard strap. This is pocket-sized fashion at its best—a neat, no-fuss wardrobe essential, pretty, yet practical.

1 Trace the pattern from the pull-out sheets provided, remembering to transfer all balance marks. Cut two skirt fronts, two front facings, two front waistbands, four front/back bibs, two back skirts, two side extensions, two back waistbands, and eight shoulder ties.

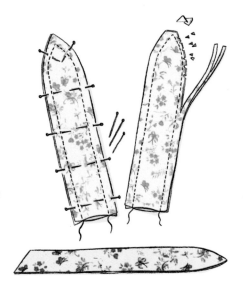

2 With right sides together and aligning the edges, pin, baste (tack), and machine stitch around all four shoulder ties, leaving the short end open. Trim off ¼ in. (5 mm) from the seam allowance and cut out little wedges around the tip. Turn right side out and press.

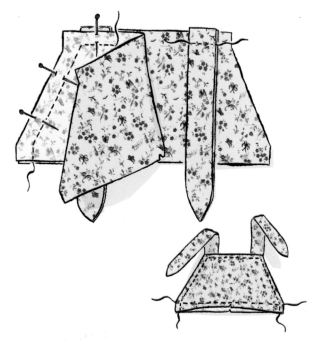

You will need:

- Pattern F: skirt front (F9), front facing (F2), front waistband (F3), front/back bib (F4), skirt back (F10), side extension (F6), back waistband (F7), and shoulder tie (F11)
- 21½-in. (55-cm) piece of 54-in. (138-cm) wide printed fabric
- Four x ¾ in. (18 mm) diameter buttons
- Matching thread

Pattern sizes: 3, 6, and **9** months

Note: Take ⅜-in. (1-cm) seam allowances throughout, unless otherwise stated

3 Pin two shoulder ties to a bib piece ⅜ in. (1 cm) in from the top side of the bib and secure with machine stitches. With right sides together and aligning the raw edges, lay another bib piece on top of the piece with the shoulder ties attached. Pin, baste (tack), and machine stitch all the way around apart from the straight lower edge. Turn right side out, press, and close the opening with a row of stay stitches. Topstitch the bib close to the edges. Repeat to make the back bib with shoulder ties.

4 With right sides facing, stitch the front skirt sections together at the center front seam. Press the seam allowance to one side, turn right side up, and topstitch close to the edge of the seam through all thicknesses. With right sides together, stitch the front facings to the front skirt pieces.

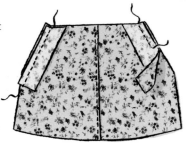

5 Turn the front facings to the inside, press, and topstitch close to the edges. With right sides facing and matching the center front notches, stitch one front waistband to the upper edge of the front skirt.

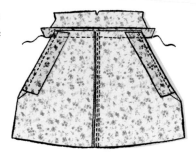

6 With right sides facing and matching the center front notches, stitch a bib to the upper edge of the front waistband. Press the seam allowance at the lower edge of the other front waistband to the wrong side and trim off the overlap. With right sides facing, stitch the two front waistband pieces together along the upper and side edges, as illustrated, ensuring that the bib is caught in between.

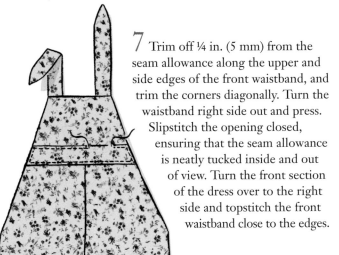

7 Trim off ¼ in. (5 mm) from the seam allowance along the upper and side edges of the front waistband, and trim the corners diagonally. Turn the waistband right side out and press. Slipstitch the opening closed, ensuring that the seam allowance is neatly tucked inside and out of view. Turn the front section of the dress over to the right side and topstitch the front waistband close to the edges.

8 To make the back section of the dress, stitch the back skirt sections together at the center back seam. Press the seam allowance to one side, turn right side up, and topstitch close to the edge of the seam through all thicknesses. With wrong sides facing, fold the side extension pieces in half and press. With right sides together, stitch them to the back skirt pieces. Press the side extensions and seam allowance away from the center of the skirt.

9 With right sides facing and matching the center back notches, stitch one back waistband to the upper edge of the back skirt. Attach the back bib and complete the back waistband in the same way as the front (see Steps 6 and 7).

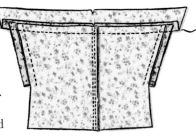

6–9 Months

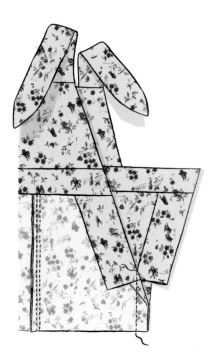

10 Lay the front and back dress sections right sides together and machine stitch together along the side seams. Start stitching at the point where the edge of the front facing and the side extension seam converge. Press the seam allowance toward the center front.

11 Stitch a double row of stitches on the front skirt section below the opening, as illustrated, to hold the side extension in place. Repeat for the other side. Make a buttonhole in each end of the front waistband and at the mid-point along the side openings, and attach buttons. Knot the shoulder ties together to finish.

Garden Miniature

9–12 MONTHS

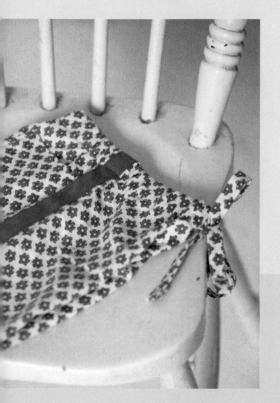

Flower Shower
Day Tripper
Wild Thing
Eastern Promise
Spring Style

Flower Shower

Liberally sprinkled with dainty woodland flowers, this enchanting little sundress in fresh candy stripe cotton is so carefree in spirit. It's also a breeze to make—only one pattern piece is required. What gives this summertime essential its extra specialness is its incredible lightness of being and the attention paid to simple, delicate detailing. Effortless enchantment guaranteed!

1 Trace pattern piece H2. Before cutting out the pattern, measure 1½ in. (4 cm) out from the straight center back edge and re-draw the center line. Measure 1¼ in. (3 cm) out from the top edge and re-draw the top line.

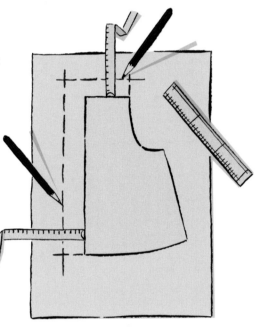

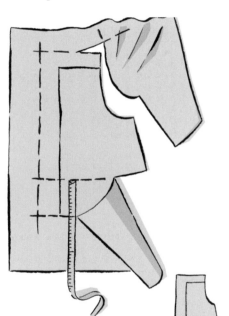

2 Measure 4¼ in. (10.5 cm) in from the bottom curved edge and re-draw the curve. Cut out the paper pattern along the re-drawn lines. Using the new pattern piece, cut out on the folded fabric two backs and two 4½ x 41-in. (11 x 104-cm) strips for the two-piece hem flounce.

You will need

- Pattern H: back (H2)
- 23½-in. (60-cm) piece of 57-in. (145-cm) wide striped fabric
- 82½ in. (210 cm) pink bias binding, ½ in. (12 mm) wide
- 31½ in. (80 cm) blue bias binding, ½ in. (12 mm) wide
- Matching thread

Pattern sizes: 12 months, 2 years, 3 years

Note: Take 3/8-in. (1-cm) seam allowances throughout, unless otherwise stated

3 With right sides facing, stitch the two backs together at the side seams and press the seams open. Machine stitch around the armholes 3/8 in. (1 cm) from the raw edge and carefully trim away the seam allowances close to the outside edge of the stitching. Bind each armhole with a 15¾-in. (40-cm) length of blue bias binding (see page 125).

4 With right sides facing, pin and machine stitch together the short edges of the two long strips of fabric to form a loop, and press the seams open. Bias bind one edge of the strip along its entire length.

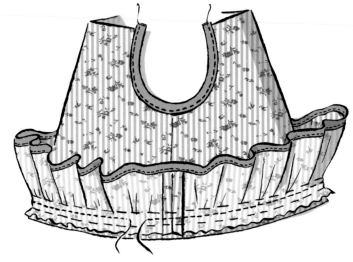

5 Gather the loop so that it is the same width as the bottom of the dress (see page 122). With right sides together, attach the gathered loop to the bottom edge of the dress, ensuring that the gathers are evenly placed all the way around. Baste (tack), then machine stitch in place.

6 Along the top edges of the dress, turn under $^3/_8$ in. (1 cm) and then another $1^1/_4$ in. (3 cm) to the inside. Pin and stitch in place, stitching close to the first folded edge to form a drawstring channel.

7 To make the shoulder ties, fold a $1^1/_2$ x $27^1/_2$-in. (4 x 70-cm) strip of fabric in half along its length and press. Open out and fold in the short ends. Fold both raw edges into the middle crease line, press, and fold in half again. Machine stitch along the length to secure the folds. Repeat for the other shoulder tie. Using a safety pin, thread one shoulder tie through one channel, one through the other channel, and tie them together in neat bows.

Day Tripper

This eclectic print of highly patterned patches is a great choice for a jolly all-weather jacket and is ideal to cut up and use for "trompe l'oeil" badges that decorate the sleeves, being somehow reminiscent of retro luggage stickers. To achieve a professional finish, provide extra warmth, and offer an additional shot of color, the drawstring hood and body are lined in vibrant cotton.

To make the windcheater

1 Using the pattern pieces provided, cut two fronts, one back, and two hoods in the print fabric. Cut two sleeves in the striped fabric. Re-using the pattern, cut two fronts, one back, two hoods, and two sleeves in the lining fabric.

2 Attach eyelets to the front hood sections in the position shown on the pattern piece. On the wrong side of the fabric, reinforce the areas with a small square of lightweight iron-on interfacing before cutting holes. Lay the hood sections right sides together and machine stitch the seam. Cut out notches along the curved seam allowance, press open, and put to one side.

3 For the sleeve appliqués, following the manufacturer's instructions, back the print fabric remnants with fusible bonding web. Cut out the motifs and apply to the sleeves (see page 125).

4 To make the pocket, cut a 4³/₄-in. (12-cm) square from the print fabric remnants. Double hem the top edge of the square by folding under ¹/₄ in. (5 mm) and then ⁵/₈ in. (1.5 cm). Stitch the fold in place. Aligning the top edges, place the template on the fabric square and wrap the excess fabric over it, steam pressing flat as you go around the template. Remove the template and trim down the excess fabric. Attach the pocket to the left front section of the windcheater as illustrated, topstitching close to the side and lower edges of the pocket.

You will need

For the windcheater
- Pattern N: front (N1), back (N2), sleeve (N3), and hood (N4)
- Jean pocket template 1
- 15³/₄-in. (40-cm) piece of 57-in. (145-cm) wide print fabric
- 13¹/₂-in. (34-cm) piece of 35¹/₂-in. (90-cm) wide stripe fabric
- 23¹/₂-in. (60-cm) piece of 57-in. (145-cm) wide lining fabric
- Lightweight iron-on interfacing
- Scraps of print fabric for appliqué details
- 8 x 8-in. (20 x 20-cm) piece of fusible bonding web
- 12-in. (30-cm) open-ended zipper fastener
- 2 metal eyelets
- 1 x 55 in. (140 cm) bootlace
- Matching thread

For the pants
- Pattern O: front (O1) and back (O2)
- Jean pocket template 2
- 23¹/₂-in. (60-cm) piece of 45-in. (112-cm) wide plain fabric
- Scraps of print fabric for waistband tabs and appliqué details
- 20¹/₂-in. (52 cm) elastic, ³/₄ in. (19 mm) wide
- 2 metal eyelets
- 1 x 55 in. (140 cm) bootlace
- Matching thread

Pattern sizes: 12 months, 2 years, 3 years

Note: Take ³/₈-in. (1-cm) seam allowances throughout, unless otherwise stated

5 With right sides together, stitch the front sections to the back section at the shoulder seams. With right sides facing, machine stitch the hood to the neck edge of the windcheater, matching the dots and center seam of the hood with the shoulder seams and center back of the jacket. Cut out notches along the curved seam allowance and press open.

6 With right sides facing, pin a sleeve to an armhole edge, matching the sleeve head and underarm balance marks with the shoulder seam and lower armhole balance mark of the jacket front. Machine stitch together, cut out notches along the curved seam allowance, and press open.

7 With right sides facing and raw edges aligned, lay the jacket front onto the jacket back and fold the sleeves in half lengthwise. Machine stitch the sleeve and side seams, and press open. Repeat Steps 2, 5, 6, and 7 to sew the jacket lining.

8 With right sides facing, pin the jacket shell to the jacket lining, matching seams and raw edges. Machine stitch together the hood edges and the lower edges of the jacket, as illustrated. Turn the jacket right side out. Fold the front edges of the jacket separately to the inside by $^5/_8$ in. (1.5 cm) and press.

9 Insert the zipper between the layers of the jacket, carefully pinning and basting (tacking) it to the layers so that the teeth are covered. Machine stitch in place. Fold separately and toward one another the lower edges of the sleeves of the jacket shell and jacket lining. Machine stitch together along the folded edge.

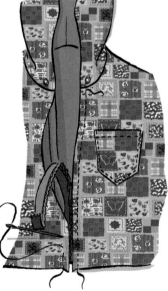

10 To create the drawstring casing for the hood, ensure that the hood layers are lying flat and machine stitch $1^1/_4$ in. (3 cm) in from the outer edge through all thicknesses from one neckline seam to the other, as illustrated. Thread the bootlace through the casing to finish.

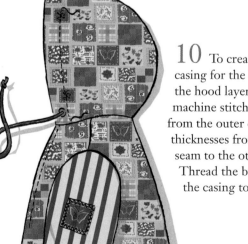

Day Tripper

To make the pants

1 Using the pattern pieces provided, cut two fronts and two backs in the plain fabric. Cut a 3 x 24-in. (8 x 61-cm) strip for the waistband.

2 To make the pockets, cut two 5¹/₂ x 6¹/₄-in. (14 x 16-cm) pieces from the fabric remnants. Double hem the top edge of one square by folding under ¹/₄ in. (5 mm) and then ⁵/₈ in. (1.5 cm). Stitch the fold in place. Aligning the top edges, place the pocket template on the fabric square and wrap the excess fabric over it, steam pressing flat as you go around the template. Remove the template and trim the excess fabric. Repeat for the other pocket.

3 For the pocket appliqués, following the manufacturer's instructions, back the print fabric remnants with fusible bonding web and apply the appliqués (see page 125). Attach the pockets to the back pant sections, as illustrated, topstitching close to the side and lower edges of the pockets.

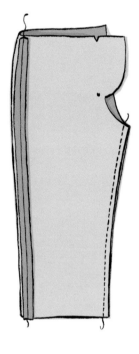

4 With right sides facing, lay the fronts on the backs and machine stitch the side seams together. Press open the seams. With right sides together, aligning the raw edges, fold each leg in half and machine stitch the inner leg seams together. Press the seams open.

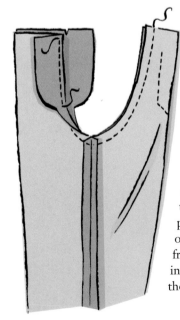

5 Turn one leg right side out and pull it into the other leg, so that the right sides are facing. With raw edges aligned, pin, baste (tack), and machine stitch along the curved center seam from the back top edge to the fly front point marked on the pattern piece. Trim the seam allowance on the curve. To create the fake fly front, fold one fly front extension to the inside along the center front line, press the fold, and edge stitch as illustrated.

6 With right sides facing, lay the outer fly front extension on the inner fly front extension and secure with machine stitches at the upper edges. Using the curved edges as a stitching guide, machine stitch the extensions together through all thicknesses, as illustrated.

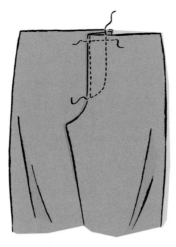

7 To make the waistband, machine stitch together the short ends of the fabric strip to create a loop. Press open the seam. With right sides facing, pin, baste (tack), and machine stitch the waistband to the upper edge of the pants, matching the waistband seam with the center back seam of the pants.

8 To make the casing for the elastic, hem the remaining raw edge by folding over $^3/_8$ in. (1 cm) and then $1^1/_4$ in. (3 cm) to the wrong side, and press. Pin, baste (tack), and edge stitch the casing in place, leaving a gap in the stitching to insert elastic. Thread elastic through the casing, adjusting it to fit the waist comfortably. Sew the ends together and stitch the opening closed.

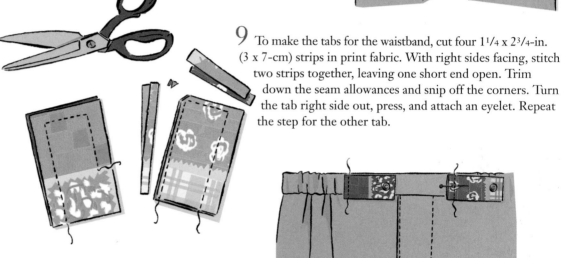

9 To make the tabs for the waistband, cut four $1^1/_4$ x $2^3/_4$-in. (3 x 7-cm) strips in print fabric. With right sides facing, stitch two strips together, leaving one short end open. Trim down the seam allowances and snip off the corners. Turn the tab right side out, press, and attach an eyelet. Repeat the step for the other tab.

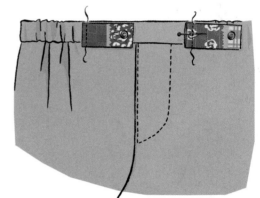

10 With the open end toward the center front of the pants, pin a tab to the waistband and machine stitch it in place through all thicknesses. Fold the tab back on itself and topstitch through all thicknesses. Repeat for the other tab. To finish, thread a 22-in. (56-cm) length of bootlace through the eyelets and tie in a neat bow. On each pant leg, press a $^5/_8$-in. (1.5-cm) hem to the inside and machine stitch in place.

Day Tripper

Wild Thing

Designed for the intrepid pint-sized explorer, this smart safari gilet has all the right components a little one needs for his big adventure. There are multiple pockets to store his little discoveries and a drawstring waist to keep him snug. A traditional block-printed Indian cotton, used for the shorts and the lining of the gilet, adds dimension to the cheeky, water-blowing elephant appliqué.

To make the gilet

1 Using the pattern pieces provided, cut two front pieces, one back piece, and two of each pocket in the plain fabric. Cut two 1½ x 23½-in. (4 x 60-cm) strips (for the drawstring), a 2¾ x 25¼-in. (7 x 64-cm) strip (for the drawstring casing), and two 1½ x 15-in. (4 x 38-cm) strips (cut on the bias) for the armhole bindings.

2 Re-using the pattern, cut two front pieces and one back piece for the lining in the print fabric. Fix the strip of interfacing to the wrong side of the front lining section that will hold the buttonholes.

3 Use the remnants of the contrast print fabric and the assorted scraps to make the appliqué details (see page 125). Apply the Elephant motif to the back section of the gilet. Embroider a tail in backstitch.

4 Make "contour-stitched" patch pockets (see page 124) and attach to the front sections of the gilet. With right sides together, stitch the front sections to the back section at the side seams.

5 Double hem the short ends of the drawstring casing by folding over ¼ in. (5 mm) and then another ¼ in. (5 mm) to the wrong side, and topstitch the folds in place. With wrong sides together, fold the casing in half lengthwise. Aligning the raw edges, pin, baste (tack), and machine stitch it to the lower edge of the gilet, ensuring that the halfway point of the casing matches up with the center back of the gilet.

Wild Thing

You will need

For the gilet

- Pattern I: front (I1) and back (I2)
- Pocket patterns 1 and 2
- Wild Thing elephant appliqué motif
- 17¾-in. (45-cm) piece of 57-in. (145-cm) wide plain fabric
- 13¾ x 35½ in. (35 x 90 cm) print fabric
- Scraps of contrast fabric for appliqué details
- 6¼ x 8 in. (16 x 20 cm) fusible bonding web
- 2 x 8¾ in. (5 x 22 cm) medium iron-on interfacing
- Three x ¾ in. (20 mm) diameter buttons
- Matching thread
- Embroidery floss (thread)

For the shorts

- Pattern J: front (J1) and back (J2)
- Pocket pattern 3
- 17¾ x 40 in. (45 x 100 cm) print fabric
- 1½ x 30 in. (4 x 76 cm) plain fabric
- 19 in. (48 cm) elastic, ¾ in. (20 mm) wide
- Matching thread

Pattern sizes: 12 months, 2 years, 3 years

Note: Take ⅜-in. (1-cm) seam allowances throughout, unless otherwise stated

6 With right sides together, stitch the front sections to the back sections at the shoulder seams. Repeat Steps 4 (without the pockets) and 6 for the gilet lining.

7 With right sides together, pin and baste (tack) the lining to the gilet, matching the centers and the side seams. Machine stitch all the way around the edges, leaving a gap in one center front edge. Trim the seam allowances, cut off the corners, and snip the curved edges. Turn the gilet right side out through the gap. Fold in the seam allowance around the gap, carefully press the finished edges, and topstitch around the neck, front, and hem.

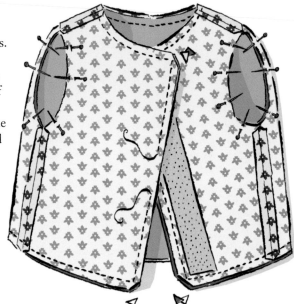

8 Carefully align the raw edges of the armholes and hold in place with basting (tacking) stitches. Stay stitch together ³/₈ in. (1 cm) from the edges. Trim the seam allowances close to the outside edge of the stitching and bind each armhole with matching fabric (see page 125). Make machine buttonholes and attach buttons to the front.

9 To make the drawstring, sew the two 1¹/₂ x 23¹/₂-in. (4 x 60-cm) fabric strips together to create one long piece. Fold in half along its length and press. Open out and fold in the short ends. Fold both raw edges into the middle crease line, press, and fold in half again. Machine stitch along the length to secure the folds. Using a safety pin, thread the drawstring through the casing at the bottom edge of the gilet.

To make the shorts

1 Using the pattern pieces provided, cut two fronts, two backs, and two pockets in the print fabric. Make the "contour-stitched" patch pockets (see page 124). Pin and baste (tack) a pocket to the back leg, topstitching close to the side and lower edges of the pocket. Repeat for the other leg.

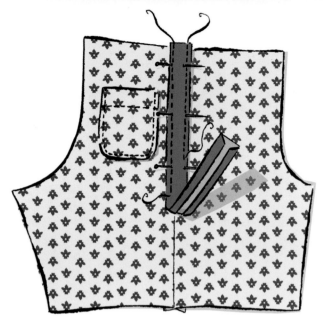

2 With right sides together, lay the fronts on the backs and machine stitch the side seams together. Press open the seams. Turn under 3/8 in. (1 cm) along both long edges of the 1 1/2 x 30-in. (4 x 76-cm) length of plain fabric and press. Cut the strip in half and pin a piece over the side seam of each leg. Edge stitch the strips in place.

3 With right sides together, aligning the raw edges, fold each leg in half and machine stitch the inner leg seams together. Press the seams open. Turn one leg right side out and pull it into the other leg, so that the right sides are facing. With raw edges aligned, pin, baste (tack), and machine stitch along the entire curved center seam from the front top edge to the back top edge. Trim the seam allowance and snip the curved edges.

4 To make the casing for the elastic waistband, double hem the top edge by folding over 3/8 in. (1 cm) and another 1 in. (2.5 cm), and press. Pin, baste (tack), and edge stitch the casing in place, leaving a gap in the stitching to insert elastic. Thread elastic through the casing, adjusting it to fit the waist comfortably. Sew the ends together and stitch the opening closed.

5 Cut a 1 1/2 x 23 1/2-in. (4 x 60-cm) strip for the fake drawstring. Fold the strip in half along its length and press. Open out and fold in the short ends. Fold both raw edges into the middle crease line, press, and fold in half again. Machine stitch along the length to secure the folds. Machine stitch the middle of the drawstring to the top center front waist through all thicknesses and tie it in a neat bow. On each pant leg, press a 5/8-in. (1.5-cm) hem to the inside and machine stitch in place.

Wild Thing

Eastern Promise

This playful two-piece is a breeze to make, is as light as a feather in floaty cotton cheesecloth (muslin), and is guaranteed to keep your little princess cool and comfy all day long. Inspired by the fables of the "Arabian Nights," the enchanting camisole top and full cut pants are embellished with richly exotic borders.

To make the camisole

1 Using the pattern pieces provided, cut two fronts, one back, and one 1³/₄ x 27-in. (4.5 x 68-cm) strip for the shoulder straps. Cut two flounces (front and back) on the center fold of the fabric. Remember to transfer all pattern markings onto the relevant fabric pattern pieces and snip into the seam allowances at the center fronts and center backs. With right sides facing, fold the strip in half lengthwise and machine stitch along the long edge, leaving the ends open. Trim away ¹/₄ in. (5 mm) of the seam allowance, turn right side out, and press. Cut the strip into two equal lengths for the shoulder straps.

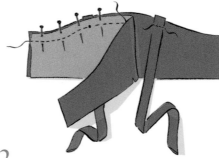

2 Lay one camisole front right side up on your work surface and attach the shoulder straps at the dot positions and at a slight angle, as illustrated. With right sides facing and aligning the upper edges, pin the remaining front on top and machine stitch together along the upper edge.

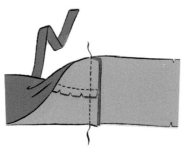

3 Trim the seam allowance, cut out little wedges in the curves, turn the front bodice right side out, and press. Open out the front section of the camisole, and with right sides facing, attach the back section at the side seams. Put to one side.

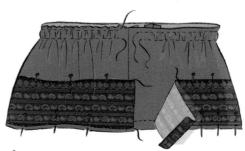

4 To make the lower section of the camisole, with right sides facing, machine stitch the two flounce pieces together at the side seams and press open the seams. Double hem the bottom edge, folding under by ¹/₄ in. (5 mm) and again by ³/₈ in. (1 cm). Pin the length of sari ribbon to the right side of the flounce and attach with small, zigzag stitches. Neatly fold under and machine stitch one end of the ribbon over the other at one side seam. Gather the upper edge of the flounce so that it is the same length as the bottom edge of the bodice section (see page 122).

You will need:

For the camisole:
- Pattern K: front (K1), back (K2), and front/back flounce (K3)
- 21¹/₄-in. (54-cm) piece of 55-in. (140-cm) wide plain fabric
- 47¹/₄ in. (120 cm) sari ribbon, 2¹/₄ in. (6 cm) wide
- 10¹/₄ in. (26 cm) elastic, 1 in. (25 mm) wide
- Matching thread

For the pants:
- Pattern Q: front/back (Q1)
- 31¹/₂-in. (80-cm) piece of 55-in. (140-cm) wide plain fabric
- 27¹/₂ in. (70 cm) sari ribbon, 2¹/₄ in. (6 cm) wide
- 19 in. (48 cm) elastic, ¹/₂ in. (12 mm) wide
- Matching thread

Pattern sizes: 12 months, 2 years, and 3 years

Note: Take ³/₈ in. (1 cm) seam allowances throughout, unless otherwise stated

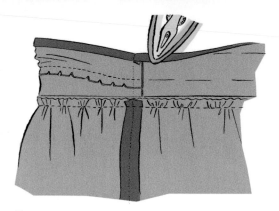

5 With right sides facing and matching all front and back center notches, attach the flounce to the bodice, remembering to match the side seams. Press the seam allowance up and toward the inside of the bodice section. Fold under ³⁄₈ in. (1 cm) and press the raw edges of the inside pieces of the front and back bodice.

6 On the inside of the camisole, carefully pin and baste (tack) the pressed edges over the seam. On the outside, carefully machine stitch through all thicknesses, along the seam where the bodice and flounce meet. Leave a gap in the stitching to insert elastic. Cut the elastic to the required length and insert into the back of the camisole through the opening. To anchor the elastic, stitch through the side seam grooves (and through all thicknesses), remembering to extend both ends of the elastic approximately ⁵⁄₈ in. (1.5 cm) beyond the side seams. Stitch the opening closed.

7 Matching the dots, pin the loose ends of the shoulder straps to the inside of the camisole back, remembering to adjust the straps to the required length before hand sewing in place.

To make the pants

1 The paper pattern for the pants requires modification before cutting out: the waistline needs to be extended in order to create fullness around the waist and hip, and an ankle cuff paper pattern is also required. Trace pattern piece Q1 from the pull-out sheets provided and cut out. Measure 2¾ in. (7 cm) up from the bottom straight edge and draw a horizontal line across the pattern at this point. Carefully cut off this strip, which will be used for the ankle cuff. Add a ³⁄₈-in. (1-cm) seam allowance to the upper edge of the strip, as illustrated.

2 Lay the shortened pants pattern on your work surface and divide it into six pieces by measuring six equal distances along the bottom edge. Carefully cut along the dividing lines, stopping short of the bottom edge.

3 Carefully lay the spliced pattern on top of a new piece of tracing paper. Increase the waist and hip measurement by gently fanning out the pattern. Measuring from the top edge, open each split by 2¼ in. (6 cm), keeping the strips flat and in position with small pieces of masking tape, which is easy to reposition. Continue the curved line of the waist by filling in the gaps between the cut strips with a pencil line. Add a ³⁄₈-in. (1-cm) seam allowance to the bottom curved edge and carefully cut out the pattern piece. If you intend to re-use the pattern, it is advisable to trace the modified pattern onto a new piece of tracing paper.

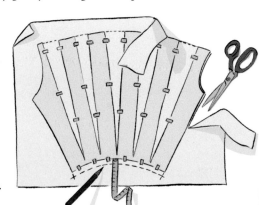

4 Using the modified pattern pieces, cut two pants, two ankle cuffs (cut on the fold), and a 1½ x 19¾-in. (4 x 50-cm) strip for the waist tie. With wrong sides facing, fold an ankle cuff in half lengthwise, press in a crease, and open out. Above the crease, pin a 13¾-in. (35-cm) length of sari ribbon to the upper right side of the cuff. Attach the ribbon to the cuff with small, zigzag stitches. Repeat for the other cuff.

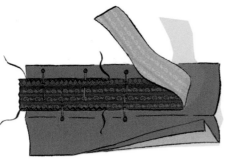

5 Stay stitch the bottom of a pant leg ⅜ in. (1 cm) in from the cut edge and carefully snip the seam allowance without cutting into the stitching line. With right sides facing, pin the ankle cuff to the pant leg, straightening out the bottom edge of the pant as you go. Machine stitch the cuff to the pant leg, using the stay stitching line as a guide.

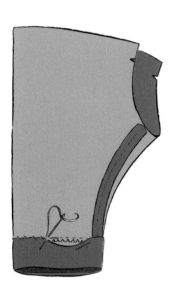

6 With right sides facing, aligning the raw edges, fold one pant leg in half and machine stitch the side seams together. Press open the seams. Fold over the ankle cuff and hand stitch the pressed edges over the seam. Repeat Steps 5 and 6 for other pant leg.

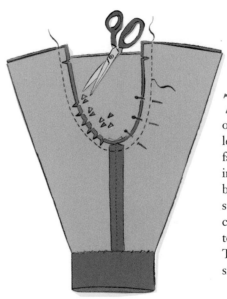

7 Turn one leg right side out and pull it into the other leg, so that the right sides are facing. With raw edges and inside leg seams aligned, pin, baste (tack), and machine stitch along the entire curved center seam from the front top edge to the back top edge. Trim the seam allowance and snip the curves.

8 Turn the pants inside out and double hem the top edge to create the casing for the elastic by folding over by ¼ in. (5 mm) and then by ¾ in. (2 cm). Pin, baste (tack), and edge stitch the casing in place, leaving a gap in the stitching to insert elastic. Thread elastic through the casing, adjusting it to fit the waist comfortably. Sew the ends together and stitch the opening closed.

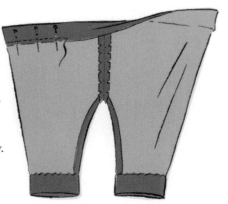

9 To make the waist tie, fold the 1½ x 19¾-in. (4 x 50-cm) strip of fabric in half along its length, press, and open out. Re-fold both edges into the middle crease line, press, and fold in half again. Topstitch close to the edge and along the entire length of the tie to secure the folds. Neaten the ends of the tie by folding under and securing with a few stitches. Sew the middle of the tie to the top center front waist through all thicknesses and tie it in a neat bow to finish.

Eastern Promise

Spring Style

This toddler's two-piece is as fresh as a daisy and its beauty is all in the detail. The crisp little blouse features a dainty, rounded collar, bishop sleeves, and an adjustable drawstring waist. The pants are detailed with a bonnie braid-trimmed hip yoke, trompe l'oeil pockets, and potted seedling appliqués. Terrific together, both items would look just as good worn separately, with a pair of faded blue jeans or a basic tee.

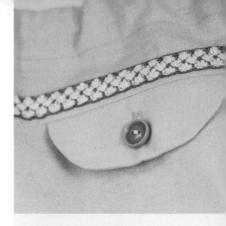

To make the blouse

1 Using the pattern pieces provided, cut two front sections (left and right), one back section, two sleeves, two collars (upper and under), and a $1\frac{1}{2}$ x 23-in. (4 x 60-cm) strip for the drawstring waist channel. Round off the collar tips using the curved edge of an eggcup and transfer all pattern markings onto the fabric before removing the paper pattern pieces.

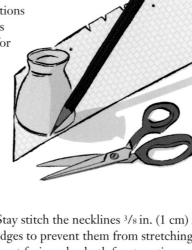

2 Stay stitch the necklines $\frac{3}{8}$ in. (1 cm) in from the cut edges to prevent them from stretching. To make the front facings, lay both front sections wrong side up on your work surface. Turn the front edges to the wrong side by $1\frac{1}{4}$ in. (3 cm), press, and secure with basting (tacking) stitches. Turn the front edges to the right side by $1\frac{1}{4}$ in. (3 cm) and secure with pins. Taking one front section, make a 90° angle at the neck edge by stitching from the folded edge to the dot and up to the upper edge. Trim away the seam allowance and carefully clip into the stitched corner. Remove the basting and turn the front facing right side out and press. Repeat for the other front section.

3 Make five buttonholes spaced evenly from the top neck to the bottom edge in the facing of the right front section and put to one side.

You will need

For the blouse

- Pattern L: front (L1), back (L2), sleeve (L3), and collar (L4)
- 19-in. (48-cm) piece of 57-in. (145-cm) wide print fabric
- 47 in. (120 cm) braid, $\frac{3}{8}$ in. (10 mm) wide
- 14 in. (36 cm) elastic, $\frac{1}{4}$ in. (5 mm) wide
- Five x $\frac{1}{2}$ in. (12 mm) diameter matching buttons
- Matching thread

For the pants

- Pattern M: front (M1), front hip yoke (M2), back (M3), and back hip yoke (M4)
- Pocket pattern 1
- Spring Style appliqué motif
- $16\frac{1}{2}$-in. (42-cm) piece of 57-in. (145-cm) wide plain fabric
- Scraps of print fabric for appliqué shapes
- $25\frac{1}{2}$ in. (65 cm) braid, $\frac{3}{8}$ in. (10 mm) wide
- 19 in. (48 cm) elastic, $\frac{3}{4}$ in. (20 mm) wide
- Two x $\frac{1}{2}$ in. (12 mm) diameter matching buttons
- Matching thread

Pattern sizes: 12 months, 2 years, 3 years

Note: Take $\frac{3}{8}$-in. (1-cm) seam allowances throughout, unless otherwise stated

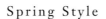

4 Fold the short ends of the strip of fabric for the drawstring waist channel over to the wrong side by ³/₈ in. (1 cm) and press. Fold the long edges of the strip over to the wrong side by ³/₈ in. (1 cm), so that they meet in the middle, and press.

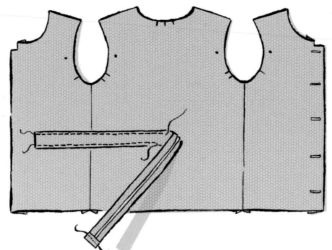

5 With right sides together, stitch the front sections to the back section at the side seams. Press open the seams, open out the blouse and lay it right side up on your work surface. Place the waist channel on top of the blouse approximately 5 in. (13 cm) above the bottom raw edge. Pin, baste (tack), and machine stitch in place, remembering to leave the ends open for the drawstring.

6 With right sides together, stitch the front sections to the back section at the shoulder seams. Make and attach the collar (see page 123). Using the longest stitch length, machine stitch ³/₈ in. (1 cm) inside and along the top edges of the sleeves between the balance marks in readiness for easing them into the armholes. With right sides together, fold the sleeves lengthwise, align the raw edges, and stitch the underarm seams. Press open the seams.

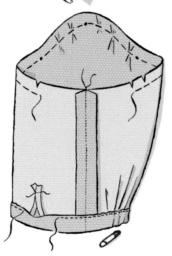

7 To double hem the sleeves, turn the bottom edges over to the wrong side by ¹/₄ in. (5 mm) and again by ³/₈ in. (1 cm). Pin, baste (tack), and machine stitch as close as possible to the folded edge, leaving a gap in the stitching to insert elastic. Using a safety pin, feed a 7-in. (18-cm) length of elastic through the channel in the sleeve. Machine stitch the ends of the elastic together, push it completely into the channel, and machine stitch the opening closed. Repeat for the other sleeve. Attach the sleeves (see page 123).

8 To double hem the blouse, turn the bottom edge over to the wrong side by ¹/₄ in. (5 mm) and again by ³/₈ in. (1 cm). Pin, baste (tack), and machine stitch as close as possible to the folded edge. Attach buttons to the front of the blouse and, using a safety pin, thread the length of braid through the waist channel.

To make the pants

1 Using the pattern pieces, cut two front pant sections and two front hip yokes (left and right), two back pant sections and two back hip yokes (left and right), and four pocket flaps. Transfer all pattern markings onto the fabric before removing the paper pattern pieces.

2 Lay two pocket flap pieces right sides together and machine stitch along the curved edge. Clip the curve, turn right side out, and press. Topstitch along the curved edge and make a buttonhole in the flap. Repeat for the other pocket flap.

9–12 Months

3 Lay a pocket flap on the right side of a front pant section, ensuring it is in a central position. Aligning the raw edges, pin, baste (tack), and machine stitch the flap in place. With right sides together, pin, baste, and machine stitch a front hip yoke to the front leg section. Press the seam allowances toward the yoke and topstitch along the seam. Repeat for the other front pant section.

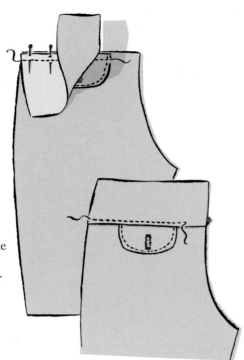

4 With right sides together and aligning the raw edges, pin, baste (tack), and machine stitch a back hip yoke to a back leg section. Press the seam allowances toward the yoke and topstitch along the seam. Repeat for the other back pant section. With right sides together, lay the pants fronts on the pants backs and machine stitch the side seams together. Press open the seams.

5 Make the appliqué shapes with scraps of leftover blouse fabric (see page 125). Appliqué a motif to the side of each leg as illustrated and sew lengths of braid across the hips, just above the seam where the pant leg joins the hip yoke.

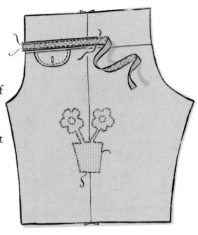

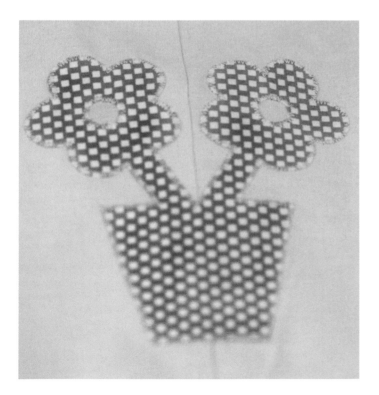

6 With right sides together, aligning the raw edges, fold each leg in half and machine stitch the inner leg seams. Press open the seams. Turn one leg right side out and pull it into the other leg, so that the right sides are facing. With raw edges aligned, pin, baste (tack), and machine stitch along the entire curved center seam from the front top edge to the back top edge. Trim the seam allowance and snip the curves.

7 To make the casing for the elastic waistband, double hem the top edge by folding over 3/8 in. (1 cm) and another 1 in. (2.5 cm), and press. Pin, baste (tack), and edge stitch the casing in place, leaving a gap in the stitching to insert elastic. Thread elastic through the casing, adjusting it to fit the waist comfortably. Sew the ends together and stitch the opening closed. Attach buttons to the front of the pants and button up the flaps.

8 To double hem the pants, turn the bottom edge over to the wrong side by ¼ in. (5 mm) and again by 3/8 in. (1 cm). Pin, baste (tack), and machine stitch as close as possible to the folded edge.

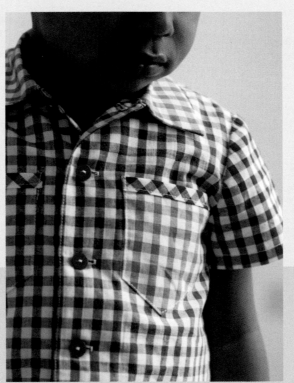

2 YEARS

Cookie-cutter Cutie

This delightful, retro-pinafore evokes a sense of reassuringly blissful domesticity. Maybe it's the wholesome tablecloth check used for the mock petticoat, the simple graphic cookie-cutter shapes of the Scandinavian-style appliqués, or perhaps the button trims and naive needlework. Playful and carefree, this is perfect for a picnic or summer fête.

1 Trace the pattern. Before cutting out the pattern pieces, measure 4¹/₄ in. (10.5 cm) in from the bottom curved edges and re-draw the curves. Cut out the paper pattern along the re-drawn lines. Using the new pattern pieces, cut two backs, two fronts, and two 3³/₄ x 36¹/₂-in. (9.5 x 93-cm) strips for the two-piece flounce in the main fabric. Cut two 5 x 36¹/₂-in. (12.5 x 93-cm) strips for the two-piece lining flounce in check fabric.

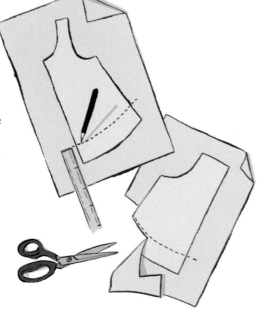

2 Back the pieces of red fabric and scraps of check fabric with fusible bonding web following the manufacturer's instructions. Create and apply the appliqué motifs (see page 125), reserving two tree shapes. Once both outer dress panels have been appliquéd, embellish the motifs with buttons and embroidery.

3 With right sides facing, machine stitch the two outer dress panels together at one side seam and press the seam open. Appliqué a tree motif over the side seam and embroider with backstitches. Repeat for the other side. Put to one side. With right sides facing, machine stitch the two dress linings together at the side seams, press the seams open, and put to one side.

You will need

- Pattern H: front (H1) and back (H2)
- Cookie-cutter Cutie appliqué motifs 1–3
- 37¹/₂-in. (95-cm) piece of 57-in. (145-cm) wide main fabric and lining
- 10¹/₄-in. (26-cm) piece of 57-in. (145-cm) wide check fabric
- 4³/₄ x 15³/₄ in. (12 x 40 cm) piece of plain red fabric
- Fusible bonding web
- 74³/₄ in. (190 cm) ready-made scalloped trim
- White embroidery floss (thread)
- Twelve x ³/₈ in. (10 mm) diameter red buttons
- Two x ¹/₂ in. (18 mm) diameter red buttons
- Matching thread

Pattern sizes: 12 months, **2 years**, 3 years

Note: Take ³/₈-in. (1-cm) seam allowances throughout, unless otherwise stated

4 With right sides facing, pin and machine stitch together the two lengths of main fabric to form a loop. Press open the seams. Fold under ⅝ in. (1.5 cm) along one long edge, pin the length of ready-made scalloped trim to the underside, and baste (tack) and machine stitch in place, neatly finishing the join in the trim.

5 Gather the loop into a flounce the same width as the bottom of the dress (see page 122). With right sides together, attach the flounce to the bottom edge of the dress, ensuring that the gathers are evenly placed all the way around. Baste (tack) in place and then machine stitch.

6 With right sides facing, pin and machine stitch together the two lengths of check fabric to form a loop. Press open the seams. Double hem the loop, turning the bottom edge over to the wrong side by ¼ in. (5 mm) and over again by ⅜ in. (1 cm). Pin, baste (tack), and machine stitch as close as possible to the folded edge.

7 Gather the check loop into a flounce the same width as the bottom of the dress lining (see page 122). Attach the right side of the flounce to the wrong side of the bottom edge of the dress lining, ensuring that the gathers are evenly placed all the way around. Baste (tack) in place and then machine stitch.

8 With right sides together, pin the lining to the dress, matching the side seams. Machine stitch all the way around the bib, armholes, and shoulder straps. Carefully trim away the seam allowances, snip the corners, and clip the curved edges. Turn the lining to the inside, carefully bag out the shoulder straps, and press. Topstitch the pressed edges of the dress in one continuous action.

9 Make a buttonhole in each top corner of the back, starting ⅝ in. (1.5 cm) down from the top edge, and sew a button to each shoulder strap.

2 Years

Ship Shape

Get set for beach or bedtime with this versatile outfit, guaranteed to become a favorite in any child's wardrobe. Loosely based on the traditional fisherman's smock, the sailor tunic top has a simple, edge-to-edge neckline and jaunty drawstring waist. The pajama-striped panel detail is repeated at the waist of the stylish trousers and also appears as a contrast hem facing, when the pant legs are worn with turn-ups.

To make the tunic top

1 Using the pattern pieces provided, cut two fronts, one back (on centerfold of fabric), and two sleeves in the striped fabric. Cut two collars (on centerfold of fabric), two 4³/₄ x 15³/₄-in. (12 x 40-cm) panels and two 4 x 5-in. (10 x 13-cm) pieces (for the patch pockets) in the plain fabric. To make the split front, with right sides facing, stitch together the two front sections of the tunic along the center front seam, 7 in. (18 cm) along from the bottom edge and ⁵/₈ in. (1.5 cm) in from the raw edge.

2 Press open the center front seam, fold over ⁵/₈ in. (1.5 cm) of the remaining unstitched seam allowance, and neaten the raw edges by folding under ¹/₄ in. (5 mm). Press, baste (tack), and machine stitch along the folded edges through all thicknesses.

3 To make the decorative horizontal bands for the front and back of the tunic, fold over the longer edges of both panels of plain fabric to the wrong side by ³/₈ in. (1 cm) and press. Place one of the bands right side up on top and across the front section of the right side of the tunic, with its lower edge approximately 3 in. (8 cm) above the raw edge of the tunic. Pin, baste (tack), and machine stitch in place. Repeat to attach the other band to the back of the tunic.

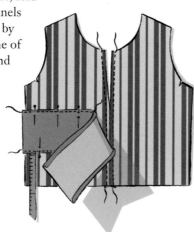

4 To make the pockets, press under the top edge of one of the 4 x 5-in. (10 x 13-cm) pieces of plain fabric by ³/₈ in. (1 cm). Turn the top edge back on itself by ¾ in. (2 cm) to form a facing. Using color-matched thread, stitch around the pocket piece along the ³/₈-in. (1-cm) seam allowance line. Turn the facing to the inside and turn under the raw edges along the stitched line, neatly folding under the corners.

You will need

For the tunic top:
- Pattern N: front (N1), back (N2), sleeve (N3), and collar (N5)
- Ship Shape appliqué anchor motif
- 9-in. (23-cm) piece of 57-in. (145-cm) wide plain fabric
- 22-in. (56-cm) piece of 57-in. (145-cm) wide striped fabric
- Scrap of white cotton fabric
- Fusible bonding web
- Medium iron-on interfacing
- 55 in. (140 cm) piping cord, ⁵/₈ in. (15 mm) diameter
- 2 metal eyelets
- Matching thread

For the pants
- Pattern M: front (M1), front hip yoke (M2), back (M3), and back hip yoke (M4)
- 19³/₄ in. (50 cm) piece of 57-in. (145-cm) wide plain fabric
- 9-in. (23-cm) piece of 57-in. (145-cm) wide striped fabric
- 2 metal eyelets
- Lightweight iron-on interfacing
- 40 in. (100 cm) piping cord, ⁵/₈ in. (15 mm) diameter
- Matching thread

Pattern sizes: 12 months, **2 years**, 3 years

Note: Take ³/₈-in. (1-cm) seam allowances throughout, unless otherwise stated

5 To make the anchor appliqué for the pocket, take a remnant of white cotton and, following the manufacturer's instructions, back it with fusible bonding web. Cut out the motif and attach it to the right pocket (see page 125). With the front section of the tunic right side up on your work surface, center both pockets on the band, approximately 4 in. (10 cm) apart, as illustrated. Topstitch around the pockets as close as possible to the sides and lower edges.

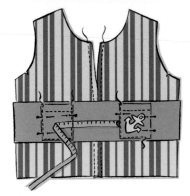

6 With right sides facing, machine stitch the front and back tunic panels together at the shoulder seams and press open. Apply iron-on interfacing to the wrong side of one of the collar pieces. Machine stitch along the notched edge, 3/8 in. (1 cm) from the edge, fold under, and press. With right sides facing, stitch the interfaced collar to the other collar piece (the under collar), leaving the notched edges open. Trim the seam allowance and snip off the corners. Turn the collar right side out, press, and put to one side.

7 Stay stitch around the entire neckline of the tunic, 3/8 in. (1 cm) in from the raw edge. Snip the seam to the stay stitching. With right sides together, raw edges aligned, and collar balance marks meeting shoulder seams, pin the under collar to the neck edge of the garment, placing the ends of the collar at the center front edges of the garment. Machine stitch in place.

8 Trim the seam allowance, snip the curves, and press the seam allowance toward the inside of the collar. Neatly hand stitch or machine stitch the pressed edge of the top collar over the neck seam.

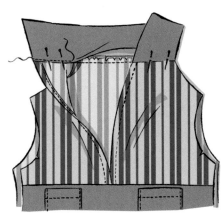

9 With right sides facing, pin a sleeve to an armhole edge, matching the sleeve notches with the front armhole notch and the shoulder. Machine stitch together, cut out wedges along the curved seam allowance, and press open. With right sides facing and raw edges aligned, lay the tunic front on the tunic back and fold the sleeves in half lengthwise. Machine stitch the sleeve and side seams, and press open.

10 Attach two eyelets to the lower center front section of the tunic, each one approximately 1½ in. (3.5 cm) in from the bottom edge and 3/4 in. (2 cm) out from the center front seam (approximately 1½ in./4 cm apart). On the wrong side of the fabric, reinforce the areas with iron-on interfacing before cutting holes.

11 To make the drawstring casing for the bottom edge of the tunic, double hem the edge by folding under 1/4 in. (5 mm) and then 3/4 in. (2 cm), and press. Pin, baste (tack), and edge stitch the casing in place. Thread the length of piping cord through the casing. Double hem the sleeves by folding under 3/8 in. (1 cm) and then 3/4 in. (2 cm), and press. Pin, baste, and machine stitch as close as possible to the folded edges.

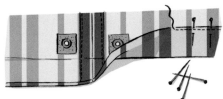

2 years

To make the pants

1 To make contrast facings for the inside of the pant legs, trace the lower section of the front leg pattern piece M1. Measure 4 in. (10 cm) up from the bottom straight edge and draw a horizontal line across the pattern at this point. Cut out the front pant facing paper pattern. Repeat the step for the back pant facing using pattern piece M3.

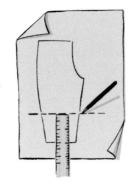

2 Using the new facing patterns together with the existing pattern pieces provided, cut two front pant sections and two back pant sections in plain fabric. Cut two front hip yokes (left and right), two back hip yokes (left and right), two front facings (left and right), and two back facings (left and right) in blue striped fabric. Remember to transfer all pattern markings onto the fabric before removing the paper pattern pieces.

3 On the wrong side of the fabric, reinforce the areas with lightweight iron-on interfacing before cutting holes. Attach eyelets to the front yoke sections in the position shown on the pattern piece.

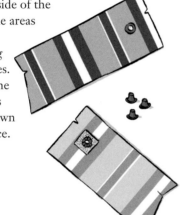

4 With right sides together and aligning the raw edges, pin, baste (tack), and machine stitch the front and back hip yokes to the front and back leg sections. Press the seam allowances toward the yokes and sew a double row of topstitching above the seam. With right sides together, lay the pant fronts on the pants backs and machine stitch the side seams together. Press the seam allowances toward the back pant and sew a double row of topstitching along the seam.

5 With right sides together, aligning the raw edges, fold each leg section in half and machine stitch the inner leg seams together. Press open the seams. With right sides together, machine stitch the left front and back facings together, along both short edges. Repeat for the right front and back facings. Fold over 3/8 in. (1 cm) of the top edge of both facings to the wrong side and press.

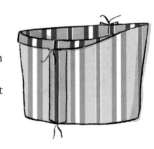

6 Pull the left pant leg into the left facing, so that the right sides are together. With the inside and outside leg seams and the bottom edges aligned, pin, baste (tack) and machine stitch the facing to the pant leg, 1/2 in (1.5cm) in from the edge and along the entire width of the pant leg.

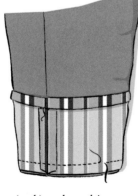

7 Turn right side out, press the hem seam and ensuring the layers are lying flat, machine stitch through all thicknesses, as close as possible to the folded edge. Repeat for the right leg. Turn one finished leg right side out and pull it into the other finished leg, so that the right sides are facing. With raw edges aligned, pin, baste (tack), and machine stitch along the entire curved center seam from the front top edge to the back top edge. Trim the seam allowance and snip the curves.

8 To make the drawstring casing for the waistband, double hem the top edge by folding over 3/8 in. (1 cm) and then by 1 in. (2.5 cm) to the wrong side, and press. Pin, baste (tack), and edge stitch the casing in place. Thread piping cord through the casing.

Shanghai Milly

Little girls will love this oriental-inspired two-piece set. The softly tailored open-front jacket with stand-up collar and tassel-trimmed "paper lantern" pockets has a delicious, shocking pink lining. What more could a little girl want? The coordinating peony print pajama pants can work well alone with a simple tee for the beach.

To make the jacket

1 Using the pattern pieces for the jacket, cut two front pieces, one back piece, two sleeves, and one collar in the main fabric. Re-using the pattern, cut two front pieces, one back piece, and one collar for the lining in contrasting fabric. Apply iron-on interfacing to the wrong side of the collar lining and a 2 x 13½-in. (5 x 34-cm) strip to the wrong side of the front lining sections that will hold the buttonholes.

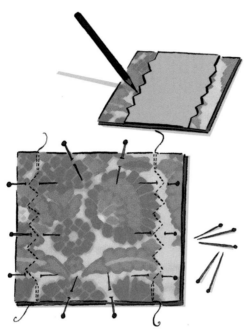

2 To make the lantern pocket, cut the floral fabric into four 5 x 6-in. (13 x 15-cm) pieces. Place the template on top of two pieces, with right sides together, and draw around the zigzag edges. Smooth the fabric so that it is free of wrinkles, pin the layers together, and carefully sew along the drawn lines. Remove the pins and carefully cut around the zigzag edges, leaving a narrow seam allowance. Snip into the corners and trim off the pointed outer edges.

3 Carefully turn the pocket right side out and press. Bind the top and bottom edges with 6-in. (15-cm) lengths of bias binding (see page 125). Fold the ends of the binding to the back of the pocket and press. Repeat for the second pocket.

4 Place the collar pieces right sides together and stay stitch all the way around, ¼ in. (5 mm) from the cut edge. Bind the top edge with a 16½-in. (42-cm) length of bias binding (see page 125). Put to one side.

You will need

For the jacket
- Pattern I: front (I1), back (I2), sleeve (I3), and collar (I4)
- Shanghai Milly lantern pocket template
- 17¾-in. (45-cm) piece of 57-in. (145-cm) wide main fabric
- 17¾-in. (45-cm) piece of 57-in. (145-cm) wide contrast fabric
- 10¼ x 12-in. (26 x 30-cm) piece of floral print fabric
- 5 x 13½-in. (12 x 34-cm) piece of medium iron-on interfacing
- 62 in. (158 cm) bias binding, 1 in. (25 mm) wide
- Two x 15¾-in. (40-cm) lengths of ³⁄₈-in. (10-mm) wide satin ribbon in two contrasting colors
- Two ready-made tassels in contrasting colors or make your own (see page 126)
- One x ¾ in. (20 mm) diameter button
- Matching thread

For the pants
- Pattern J: front (J1) and back (J2)
- Pocket pattern 4
- 23½-in. (60-cm) piece of 57-in. (145-cm) wide floral print fabric
- 58¼-in. (148 cm) bias binding, 1 in. (25 mm) wide
- 19 in. (48 cm) elastic, ¾ in. (20 mm) wide
- Matching thread

Pattern sizes: 12 months, **2 years**, 3 years
Note: Take ³⁄₈-in. (1-cm) seam allowances throughout, unless otherwise stated

Shanghai Milly

5 Lay a front section right side up on your work surface. Pin and baste (tack) a 15³/₄-in. (40-cm) length of satin ribbon to the center, carefully placing the hanging cord of a matching tassel beneath the end of the ribbon that has been folded under. Edge stitch the ribbon in place. Repeat the step to embellish the other front section.

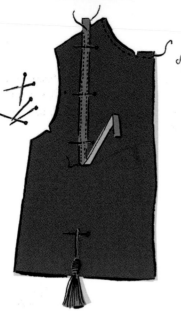

6 Pin and baste (tack) the lantern pocket to the jacket front, ensuring that the end of the ribbon is concealed and the tassel is hanging freely. Topstitch the sides and lower edge of the pocket. Repeat to attach the remaining pocket to the other front section.

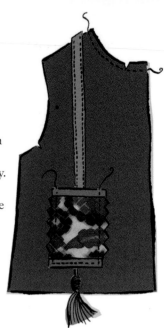

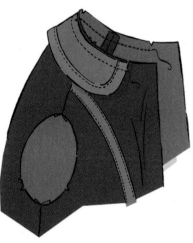

7 With right sides together, stitch the front sections to the back section at the shoulder and side seams. Matching balance marks and the dots to the shoulder seams, attach the collar.

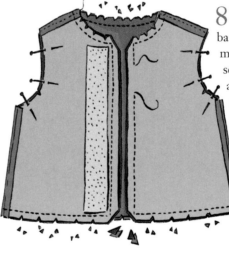

8 With right sides together, pin and baste (tack) the lining to the jacket, matching the centers and the side seams. Machine stitch all the way around the edges. Trim the seam allowances, cut off the corners, and snip the curved edges. Turn the lining to the inside through an armhole, carefully press the finished edges, and topstitch around the neck, front, and hem.

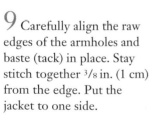

9 Carefully align the raw edges of the armholes and baste (tack) in place. Stay stitch together ³/₈ in. (1 cm) from the edge. Put the jacket to one side.

10 Trim away the 1¹/₄-in. (3-cm) hem allowance on the sleeves. Using the longest machine stitch, stitch around the sleeve heads between the balance marks in order to gather them slightly to help ease the sleeves into the armholes later. With right sides together, fold the sleeves lengthwise, align the raw edges, and stitch the underarm seams. Bind the lower edge of the sleeves with an 11-in. (28-cm) length of bias binding (see page 125). Attach the sleeves to the jacket body (see page 123). Make a machine buttonhole at the top neck and attach buttons to the front.

To make the pants

1 Using the pattern pieces for the pants, cut two fronts, two backs, and two pockets in the floral print fabric. Trim off the hem allowance at the bottom edge of the front and back pant pieces.

2 Before assembling the "contour-stitched" patch pockets (see page 124), edge stitch a 4¹/₂-in. (11-cm) length of bias binding to the upper part of each pocket.

3 Pin and baste (tack) a pocket to one front leg, topstitching close to the side and lower edges of the pocket. Repeat for other leg. With right sides together, lay the pant fronts on the pant backs and machine stitch the side seams together.

4 With right sides together, aligning the raw edges, fold each leg section in half and machine stitch the inner leg seams together. Press open the seams. Turn one leg right side out and pull it into the other leg, so that the right sides are facing. With raw edges aligned, pin, baste (tack), and machine stitch along the entire curved center seam from the front top edge to the back top edge. Trim the seam allowance and snip the curves.

5 To make the casing for the elastic waistband, double hem the top edge by folding over ³/₈ in. (1 cm) and then 1 in. (2.5 cm) to the wrong side, and press. Pin, baste (tack), and edge stitch the casing in place, leaving a gap in the stitching to insert elastic. Thread elastic through the casing, adjusting it to fit the waist comfortably. Sew the ends together and stitch the opening closed.

6 To make the fake drawstring, fold a 19³/₄-in. (50-cm) length of bias binding in half along its length and press. Open out and fold in the short ends. Re-fold and machine stitch along the length to secure the folds. Sink stitch the middle of the drawstring onto the top center front waist and tie it in a neat bow. Finish each pant leg with a 15-in. (38-cm) length of bias binding.

Shanghai Milly

Checkmate

What could be fresher for summer than gingham checks and laundered cotton? Upbeat colors, relaxed yet classic shapes, and clean-cut detailing combine for an outfit that oozes resort chic. Any parent planning a spell on the French Riviera will see that this smart little two-piece should definitely be on the *menu du jour*.

To make the shirt

1 Using the pattern pieces provided, cut two front sections (left and right) and one (under) collar in blue check, one back section and one (top) collar in lilac check, one sleeve in green check, and one sleeve and a 1¹/₂ x 14-in. (4 x 36-cm) strip (cut on the bias) in red check. Transfer all pattern markings onto the fabric before removing the paper pattern pieces. Reserve the scraps of green and lilac check fabric. Stay stitch the necklines ³/₈ in. (1 cm) in from the cut edges to prevent them from stretching.

2 To make the front facings, lay both front sections wrong side up on your work surface. Turn the center front edges 1¹/₄ in. (3 cm) to the wrong side, press, and secure with basting (tacking) stitches. Turn the center front edges 1¹/₄ in. (3 cm) to the right side and secure with pins. Taking one front section, make a 90° angle at the neck edge by stitching from the folded edge to the dot and up to the upper edge. Trim away the seam allowance and carefully clip into the stitched corner. Turn the facing right side out and press. Repeat the step for the other front section.

3 Make five buttonholes evenly spaced from the top neck to bottom edge in the facing of the left front section. Put to one side.

4 To make the shirt pockets, cut two 4³/₄-in. (12-cm) squares from the remnants of green and lilac check fabric. Make the binding by folding the red check fabric strip in half along its length and press. Open out and fold both raw edges into the middle crease line. Press, and fold in half again. Cut off two 4³/₄-in. (12-cm) lengths and bind the upper edge of the two "pocket" squares (see page 125).

5 Aligning the top edges, place the template on one fabric square and wrap the excess fabric over it, steam pressing flat as you go around the template. Remove the template and trim down the excess to ³/₈ in. (1 cm). Repeat the step for the other pocket.

Checkmate

You will need

For the shirt
- Pattern L: front (L1), back (L2), collar (L4), and sleeve (L5)
- Jean pocket template 1
- 9 x 19 in. (23 x 48 cm) lilac check fabric
- 12¹/₂ x 17¹/₄ in. (32 x 44 cm) blue check fabric
- 13¹/₂ x 13¹/₂ in. (34 x 34 cm) red check fabric
- 6¹/₄ x 15 in. (16 x 38 cm) green check fabric
- Five x ¹/₂ in. (12 mm) diameter buttons
- Matching thread

For the shorts
- Pattern M: front (M1), front hip yoke (M2), back (M3), and back hip yoke (M4)
- Pocket pattern 4
- 15-in. (38-cm) piece of 57-in. (145-cm) wide plain fabric
- 4³/₄-in. (12-cm) piece of 57-in. (145-cm) wide blue check fabric
- Lightweight iron-on interfacing
- Scraps of lilac check fabric for loops
- Four x ¹/₂ in. (12 mm) diameter buttons
- 40 in. (100 cm) piping cord, ⁵/₈ in. (15 mm) diameter
- Matching thread

Pattern sizes: 12 months, **2 years**, 3 years

Note: Take ³/₈-in. (1-cm) seam allowances throughout, unless otherwise stated

6 Attach a pocket to each front panel, using the illustration as a guide for position.

7 Using the leftover pocket binding, sew a 2-in. (5-cm) loop to the back neck, as illustrated.

8 With right sides together, stitch the front shirt sections to the back shirt section at the side and shoulder seams. Press open the seams. Make and attach the collar (see page 123). Using the longest stitch length, machine stitch 3/8 in. (1 cm) inside and along the top edges of the sleeves between the balance marks in readiness for easing them into the armholes. With right sides together, fold the sleeves lengthwise, align the raw edges, and stitch the underarm seams. Press open the seams.

9 To double hem the sleeves, turn the bottom edges over to the wrong side by 1/4 in. (5 mm) and again by 3/8 in. (1 cm). Pin, baste (tack), and machine stitch as close as possible to the folded edge. Attach the sleeves to the shirt (see page 123). To double hem the shirt, turn the bottom edge over to the wrong side by 1/4 in. (5 mm) and again by 3/8 in. (1 cm). Pin, baste, and machine stitch as close as possible to the folded edge. Attach buttons to the front of the shirt to finish.

To make the shorts

1 When tracing the front and back shorts leg patterns onto tissue paper, draw and cut on the lines that read "cut here for shorts" before pinning the pattern pieces to your fabric. Remember to transfer all pattern markings onto the fabric before removing the paper pattern pieces.

2 Using the pattern pieces, cut two front pant sections, two back pant sections, and four pockets in plain fabric. Cut two front hip yokes (left and right), and two back hip yokes (left and right) in blue check fabric. Make buttonholes in the front yoke sections at the positions shown on the pattern piece and cut them open. On the wrong side of the fabric, reinforce the areas to be sewn with lightweight iron-on interfacing.

3 With right sides together and aligning the raw edges, pin, baste (tack), and machine stitch the front and back hip yokes to the front and back leg sections. Press the seam allowances toward the yokes. With right sides together, lay the pant fronts onto the pant backs and machine stitch side the seams together. Press the seam allowances toward the back pant and topstitch along the seam.

4 Make the four "contour-stitched" patch pockets (see page 124), adding buttonholes to the upper areas. Cut open the buttonholes before attaching the pockets to the leg sections.

5 Cut a 1¹/₂ x 8-in (4 x 20-cm) strip from the lilac check fabric remnants to make two loops for the pockets. Fold the strip in half along its length and press. Open out, fold both raw edges into the middle crease line, press, fold in half again, and machine stitch as close as possible along both edges. Cut the strip in half, fold each piece into a loop as illustrated, and machine stitch to secure the folds.

6 Pin and baste (tack) the pockets to the back legs, inserting a loop beneath the lower edge of one pocket. Topstitch close to the side and lower edges of the pockets. Repeat the step for the remaining two pockets to be attached to the sides of the lower legs, again, inserting a loop beneath the lower edge of one pocket.

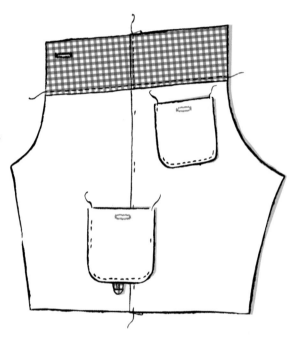

7 With right sides together, aligning the raw edges, fold each leg section in half and machine stitch the inner leg seams together. Press open the seams. Turn one leg right side out and pull it into the other leg, so that the right sides are facing. With raw edges aligned, pin, baste (tack), and machine stitch along the entire curved center seam from the front top edge to the back top edge. Trim the seam allowance and snip the curves.

8 To make the drawstring casing for the waistband, double hem the top edge by folding over ³/₈ in. (1 cm) and then 1 in. (2.5 cm), and press. Pin, baste (tack), and edge stitch the casing in place. Thread piping cord through the casing and attach buttons to the pockets. To double hem the pants, turn the bottom edge over to the wrong side by ¹/₄ in. (5 mm) and again by ³/₈ in. (1 cm). Pin, baste, and machine stitch as close as possible to the folded edge.

Tutti-frutti

I love this print, a dusty, flea-market remnant I found, lovingly restored and put to good use. It reminds me of one very similar, used for a dress made by my mum for my sister when she was very small, except the apples were little purple radishes. This dress is relatively basic; it's the cute, doll-like silhouette, prim contrast bindings, and printed sleeve bands that give it that extra something special.

You will need

- Pattern P: front sleeve (P1), bib (P2), and back bodice (P3)
- 15¾-in. (40-cm) piece of 45-in. (112-cm) wide plain fabric
- 15¾-in. (40-cm) piece of 45-in. (112-cm) wide print fabric
- 75 in. (190 cm) bias binding, ¾ in. (20 mm) wide
- Matching thread

Pattern sizes: 12 months, **2 years**, 3 years

Note: Take ³⁄₈-in. (1-cm) seam allowances throughout, unless otherwise stated

1 Using the pattern pieces provided, cut two front sleeves (left and right), two bibs (on the fold), and one back (on the fold) in plain fabric. Cut two 14½ x 20½-in. (37 x 52-cm) rectangles in print fabric for the skirt. Retain the remnants to use later as sleeve trim. Aligning the center fronts, lay the bib paper pattern on top of the wrong side of one fabric bib and carefully transfer the dots to mark the stitching line for the front slit.

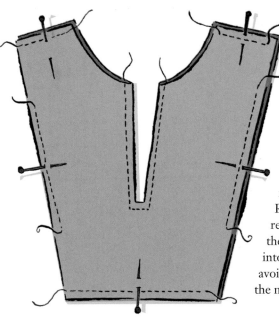

2 With right sides facing and aligning all edges, lay the bib pieces together and join the dots with machine stitches. Re-stitch the point to reinforce. Carefully cut the front slit and snip into the corners, avoiding cutting through the machine stitches.

3 Turn the bib pieces right side out and press. Topstitch the front slit and stay stitch ¼ in. (5 mm) in along the edges of the bib to keep them aligned.

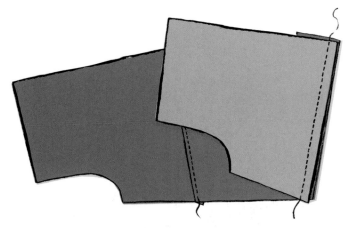

4 With right sides together, machine stitch a front sleeve to one side of the bib. Press the seam allowances toward the bib and topstitch along the seam. Repeat for the other sleeve.

Tutti-frutti

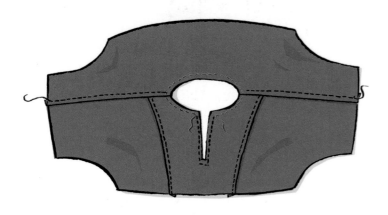

5 Stay stitch the necklines ¼ in. (5 mm) in from the cut edges to prevent them stretching during make. With right sides facing and aligning all edges, machine stitch the front and back bodice together. Press the seam allowances toward the back bodice and topstitch along the seam.

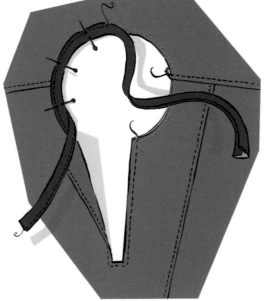

6 Lay the completed bodice right side up on your work surface. Place a 1½-in. (4-cm) wide strip of remnant print fabric on top of the bodice sleeve, 1 in. (2.5 cm) in from the edge and zigzag stitch in place. Repeat for the other sleeve.

7 Bind the neck edge in one continuous action with a 53½-in. (136-cm) length of bias binding to form the front neck ties (see page 125). With right sides facing, machine stitch the front and back bodices together at the underarm seams. Press the seams open. Bind the sleeve edges with 10¼-in. (26-cm) lengths of bias binding.

8 To make the skirt, with right sides facing, machine stitch the front and back panels together at the side seams and press the seams open. Gather the top edge of the skirt so that it is the same width as the bottom of the bodice (see page 122). With right sides together, attach the gathered skirt to the bottom edge of the bodice, ensuring that the gathers are evenly placed all the way around. Baste (tack) in place and then machine stitch. To double hem the dress, turn the bottom edge over to the wrong side by ¼ in. (5 mm) and then again by ³⁄₈ in. (1 cm). Pin, baste, and machine stitch as close as possible to the folded edge.

3 YEARS

Watch the Birdie
Dotty Duster
Lucky Seven
Prim and Proper
Peasant Dreams

Watch the Birdie

Fledgling fashionistas will find this witty "one-off" irresistible—a flattering A-line pinafore with songbirds gathering sociably round and about a cottage garden scene. The continuous binding around the neckline, armholes, and shoulder straps not only provides the perfect finish, it is also a great time-saver, removing the need to make tricky double hems along all those curved edges.

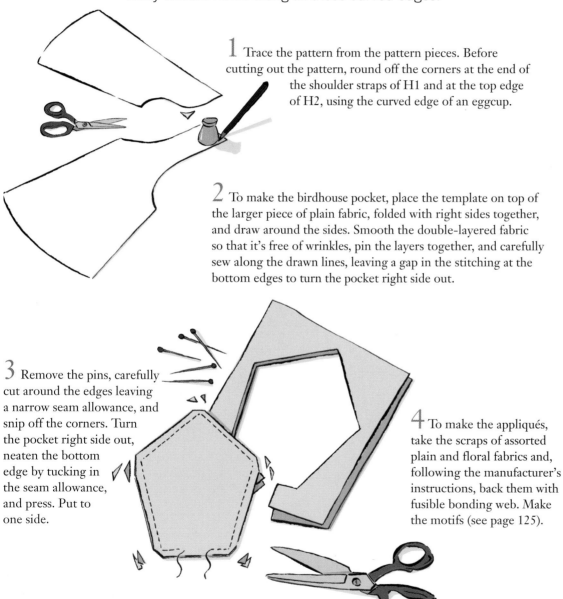

1 Trace the pattern from the pattern pieces. Before cutting out the pattern, round off the corners at the end of the shoulder straps of H1 and at the top edge of H2, using the curved edge of an eggcup.

2 To make the birdhouse pocket, place the template on top of the larger piece of plain fabric, folded with right sides together, and draw around the sides. Smooth the double-layered fabric so that it's free of wrinkles, pin the layers together, and carefully sew along the drawn lines, leaving a gap in the stitching at the bottom edges to turn the pocket right side out.

3 Remove the pins, carefully cut around the edges leaving a narrow seam allowance, and snip off the corners. Turn the pocket right side out, neaten the bottom edge by tucking in the seam allowance, and press. Put to one side.

4 To make the appliqués, take the scraps of assorted plain and floral fabrics and, following the manufacturer's instructions, back them with fusible bonding web. Make the motifs (see page 125).

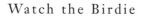

Watch the Birdie

103

You will need

- Pattern H: front (H1) and back (H2)
- Watch the Birdie birdhouse pocket template
- Watch the Birdie bird and birdhouse appliqué motifs
- 25¼-in. (64-cm) piece of 57-in. (145-cm) wide check fabric
- 5½ x 12 in. (14 x 30 cm) plain fabric for pocket
- 4 x 4 in. (10 x 10 cm) plain fabric for flowerpot
- Scraps of assorted multicolored plain and floral print fabrics for appliqué shapes
- Fusible bonding web
- 57 in. (145 cm) bias binding, ¾ in. (20 mm) wide
- Lightweight iron-on interfacing
- Two x ¾ in. (20 mm) diameter buttons
- Matching thread

Pattern sizes: 12 months, 2 years, **3 years**

Note: Take ⅜-in. (1-cm) seam allowances throughout, unless otherwise stated. In this project, the back pattern is used for the dress front and vice-versa

5 Decide on the position of the pocket (approximately 4³/4 in./ 12 cm above the raw hemline). Before attaching it to the panel, create a "sunburst" effect with the leaf appliqués, as illustrated. Continue adding to the "garden scene" with the flowerpot, shrub, and songbird appliqués. Appliqué a heart and two lovebirds to the back panel.

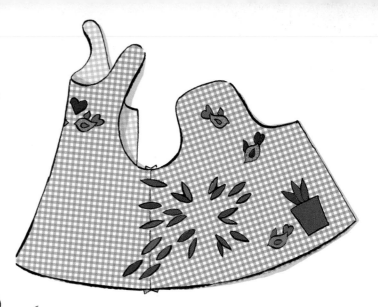

6 With right sides facing, machine stitch the two dress panels together at one side seam. Press the seam open, and appliqué leaves over the side seam and across onto the back. Appliqué the heart, spy hole, and perch to the pocket and place it in position at the center of the leaf sunburst. Pin, baste (tack), and machine stitch in place.

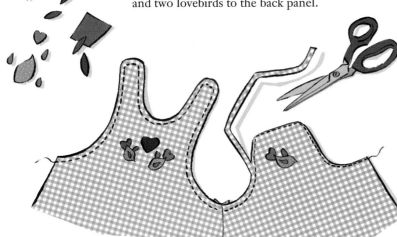

7 Machine stitch around the bib, armholes, and shoulder straps ³/8 in. (1 cm) in from the raw edge and carefully trim away the seam allowances close to the outside edge of the stitching.

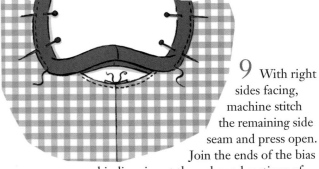

9 With right sides facing, machine stitch the remaining side seam and press open. Join the ends of the bias binding, insert the unbound sections of armhole into it, and close with machine stitches. Make a buttonhole in the end of each shoulder strap, reinforcing the underside of the area to be sewn with lightweight iron-on interfacing beforehand. Sew a button in each top corner of the bib.

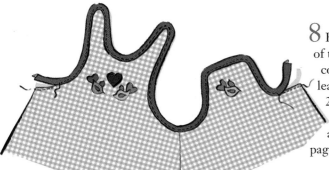

8 Bind the top edges of the dress in one continuous action, leaving approximately 2¹/2 in. (6 cm) of binding unstitched at each end (see page 125).

10 To double hem the dress, turn the bottom edge over to the wrong side by ¹/4 in. (5 mm) and then again by ³/8 in. (1 cm). Pin, baste (tack), and machine stitch as close as possible to the folded edge.

Dotty Duster

This light, loose-fitting long coat is a real entrance-maker in bold, eye-popping spotted cotton. Combining serious fashion style with wonderland whimsy, it features dainty sleeve tabs and a chic martingale back, alongside "comic creature" appliqués that pop out unexpectedly from the pocket and back vent. Make the coat in waterproof cotton to bring cheer to your little one on a rainy day.

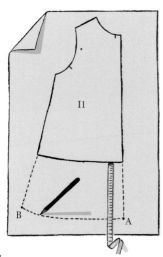

1 To lengthen the front panel, trace pattern piece I1. Extend the straight center line by 6 in. (15 cm) to A and the diagonal line at the side seam by 6 in. (15 cm) to B. Re-draw the hemline from A to B, matching the curved hemline of the original jacket pattern. Cut out the paper pattern along the re-drawn lines.

2 To make the front facing pattern, take an additional sheet of paper and trace off the central area of the new front pattern piece I1. Draw a line from the neck edge to the hemline that is parallel with and 2³/₄ in. (7 cm) in from the straight central edge. Draw a line from the shoulder edge to the straight central edge that is parallel with and 2 in. (5 cm) in from the curved neck edge. Place a round plate over the corner created by these lines so that the rim touches the two sides. Draw around the plate to round off the corner. Cut out the paper pattern along the re-drawn lines.

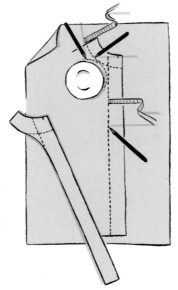

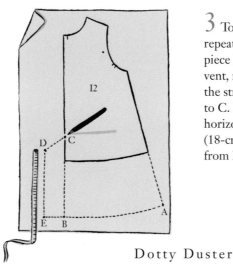

3 To lengthen the back panel, repeat Step 1, using pattern piece I2. To create the back vent, measure 8 in. (20 cm) up the straight center line from B to C. Draw a 2¹/₄-in. (6-cm) horizontal line (at a 90° angle) out from B to E and draw a 7-in. (18-cm) vertical line (at a 90° angle) from E up to D. Draw a line from D to C to complete the back vent extension.

You will need

- Pattern I: front (I1), back (I2), sleeve (I3), and collar (I5)
- Pocket pattern 5
- Dotty Duster martingale/ sleeve tab template
- Dotty Duster animal appliqué motifs
- 40-in. (100-cm) piece of 57-in. (145-cm) wide spotted fabric
- Scraps of contrast fabric for appliqué details
- Fusible bonding web
- 8 x 25¹/₄ in. (20 x 65 cm) mediumweight iron-on interfacing
- 66 in. (168 cm) bias binding, 1 in. (25 mm) wide
- Embroidery floss (thread)
- Seven x ⁷/₈ in. (18 mm) diameter buttons
- Matching thread

Pattern sizes: 12 months, 2 years, **3 years**

Note: Take ³/₈-in. (1-cm) seam allowances throughout, unless otherwise stated

Dotty Duster

4 Add a ³/₈-in. (1-cm) seam allowance to the center back by drawing a line down from the top neck edge to the diagonal line C to D. Cut out the paper pattern along the re-drawn lines.

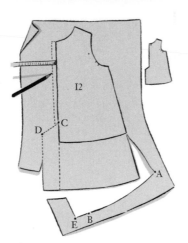

5 Using the new and modified patterns with the existing ones, cut two front sections, two front facings, two back sections, two sleeves, and two collars (upper and under) in the spotted fabric. Transfer all pattern markings onto the fabric before removing the paper pattern pieces.

6 To make the appliqués, back the scraps of contrast fabric with fusible bonding web following the manufacturer's instructions. Cut out the motifs and apply four creatures to the front sections of the coat, as illustrated (see page 125). Create the facial features with backstitches and French knots (see page 126).

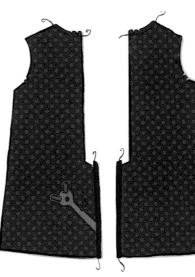

7 Apply a creature to the left back section of the coat and embroider the facial features. Pin and baste (tack) a 9-in. (23-cm) length of bias binding to both long edges of the center back vent. Edge stitch the bindings in place.

8 With right sides facing, machine stitch the back sections together, making sure that you align the vent edges. Open out the back sections and press the seam allowance and the vents in one direction. Turn the back of the coat right side up, re-press the crease, and sink stitches diagonally through all thicknesses at the upper end of the vent.

9 Make two "contour-stitched" patch pockets (see page 124). Pin and baste (tack) a pocket to the front section, topstitching close to the side and lower edges of the pocket. Repeat for the other front section, laying the pocket over the appliqué.

3 Years

10 With right sides together, stitch the coat front to the back at the shoulder and side seams and put to one side. To make the collar, apply interfacing to the wrong side of the under collar and follow the instructions on page 124. Attach the collar.

11 Apply interfacing to the wrong sides of the facings. Pin a 25¼-in. (64-cm) length of bias binding to the inner edge of each front facing. Edge stitch the bindings in place and fold under the narrow ends of the facings. With right sides together, pin the facings to the front and neck edges of the coat and machine stitch through all thicknesses. Trim the seam allowances, clip the corners, and snip the curved edges. Turn the facings to the inside and press.

12 To make the martingale, place the template on top of a 6¼ x 9½-in. (16 x 24-cm) piece of fabric, folded right sides together. Draw around the shape, pin the layers together, and carefully sew along the drawn lines, leaving a gap in the stitching at the bottom edges to turn the martingale right side out. Remove the pins, carefully cut around the edges leaving a narrow seam allowance, and snip the curved edges. Turn the martingale right side out, neatly tuck in the exposed seam allowances, press flat, and topstitch along the outer edges.

13 To make the sleeve tabs, repeat Step 12. Cut the piece into two equal lengths and put to one side together with the martingale. Using the longest machine stitch, stitch around the sleeve heads between the balance marks in order to gather them slightly and help ease them into the armholes later. Place a tab at the side of each sleeve as illustrated, pin, and machine stitch in place.

15 To hem the coat, turn the front facings and the vents to the outside. Aligning the lower edges of the coat with the lower edges of the facings, pin, baste (tack), and machine stitch along the lower edge. Trim the lower edges of the facings, snip off corners, and turn inside. Press the facings, press up a 1¼-in. (3-cm) hem, and slipstitch in place.

14 With right sides together, fold the sleeves lengthwise, align the raw edges, and stitch the underarm seams. Finish the lower edge of the sleeve with a 1¼-in. (3-cm) hem. Repeat for the other sleeve. Attach the sleeves to the coat body (see page 123).

16 Machine buttonhole the front of the coat, attach the martingale to the back and attach buttons to the front, martingale, and sleeve tabs.

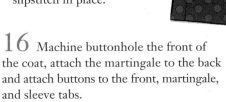

Dotty Duster

Lucky Seven

This perfect pairing is ideal for little urbanites. The playful fleece jacket is patchworked together in "jockey silks" fashion and given a high-tech twist with wetsuit-inspired detailing for the patch pockets that are repeated on the back of basic jogging pants. An oversized "Lucky Seven" appliqué is emblazoned on the front leg.

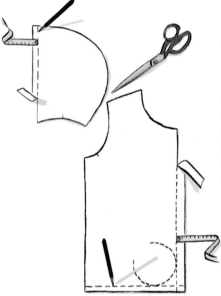

To make the hoodie

1 Trace the pattern from the pull-out sheets provided. Before cutting out the pattern pieces, draw a line ⁵/₈ in. (1.5 cm) in from the front straight edge of the hood. Cut out the paper pattern along the re-drawn line. Draw a line ⁵/₈ in. (1.5 cm) in from the straight edge of the jacket front and a line ³/₈ in. (1 cm) in from the bottom edge. Round off the corner using the rim of a tea cup. Cut out the paper pattern along the re-drawn line.

2 Draw a line ³/₈ in. (1 cm) in from the bottom edge of the jacket back and a line ³/₈ in. (1 cm) out from the straight center back edge. Draw a line ³/₈ in. (1 cm) in from the bottom edge of the sleeve, and cut out both paper pattern pieces along the re-drawn lines.

3 Using the modified pattern pieces, cut one hood piece in lilac fleece and one in plum fleece. Cut one front piece in pink fleece and one in chocolate fleece. Cut one back piece in blue fleece and one back, one sleeve, and one pocket in yellow fleece. Cut one sleeve and one pocket in turquoise fleece. Lay the two hood pieces right sides together and machine stitch the seam. Trim the seam allowance to ¹/₄ in. (5 mm) and put to one side.

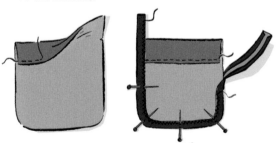

4 Take one pocket piece, fold over 1¹/₄ in. (3 cm) along the top edge, and machine stitch to secure. Bind the three remaining sides of the pocket with a 15³/₄-in. (40-cm) length of bias binding, using small zigzag stitches (see page 125). Fold under the ends of the bias binding and press. Repeat for the other pocket and put to one side.

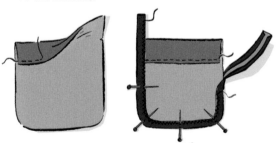

Lucky Seven

You will need

For the hoodie

- Pattern N: front (N1), back (N2), sleeve (N3), and hood (N4)
- Pocket pattern 5
- 12 x 14 in. (30 x 36 cm) lilac fleece fabric
- 12 x 14 in. (30 x 36 cm) plum fleece fabric
- 12 x 14 in. (30 x 36 cm) blue fleece fabric
- 21¼ x 23 in. (54 x 58 cm) yellow fleece fabric
- 10¼ x 18 in. (26 x 46 cm) pink fleece fabric
- 10¼ x 18 in. (26 x 46 cm) chocolate fleece fabric
- 15¾ x 20½ in. (40 x 52 cm) turquoise fleece fabric
- 11-in. (28-cm) open-ended zipper fastener
- 136¼ in. (346 cm) purple bias binding, 1 in. (25 mm) wide
- Matching thread

For the jogging pants

- Pattern O: front (O1) and back (O2)
- Pocket pattern 5
- Lucky Seven appliqué motif
- 23½-in. (60-cm) piece of 61½-in. (156-cm) wide plum fleece fabric
- 7 x 12 in. (18 x 30 cm) lilac fleece fabric
- 4¾ x 7 in. (12 x 18 cm) turquoise fleece fabric
- 31½ in. (80 cm) bias binding, 1 in. (25 mm) wide
- Fusible bonding web
- 21¼ in. (54 cm) elastic, ½ in. (12 mm) wide
- Matching thread

Pattern sizes: 12 months, 2 years, **3 years**

Note: Take ³/₈-in. (1-cm) seam allowances throughout, unless otherwise stated

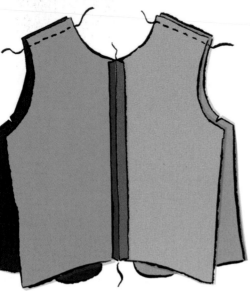

5 With right sides facing, sew the back sections together at the center back seam and sew the front sections to the back section at the shoulder seams.

6 With right sides facing, machine stitch the hood to the neck edge of the jacket, making sure you match the dots and center seam of the hood with the shoulder seams and center back of the jacket. Trim the seam allowance to 1/4 in. (5 mm). With right sides facing, pin a sleeve to an armhole edge, matching the sleeve head and underarm balance marks with the shoulder seam and lower armhole balance mark of the jacket front. Machine stitch together and trim the seam allowance to 1/4 in. (5 mm).

7 With right sides facing and raw edges aligned, lay the jacket front on the jacket back and fold the sleeves in half lengthwise. Machine stitch the sleeve and side seams, and trim the seam allowance to 1/4 in. (5 mm). Turn the jacket right side out and bind the raw edges of the jacket and hood with an 82½-in (210-cm) length of bias binding, using small zigzag stitches.

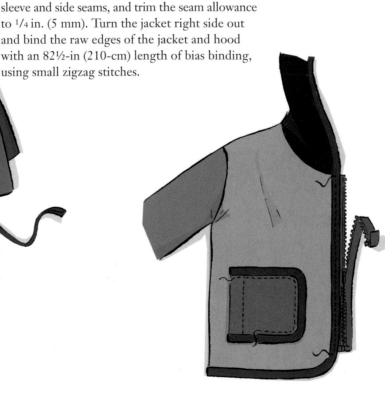

8 Attach the pockets to the front of the jacket, carefully topstitching alongside the folded inside edge of the bias binding. Lay the zipper underneath the center front edges, carefully pinning and basting (tacking) the zipper tape to the bindings so that the teeth are exposed. Machine stitch the zipper in place. Finish each sleeve edge with an 11-in. (28-cm) length of bias binding.

To make the jogging pants

1 Using the pattern pieces provided, cut two fronts and two backs in the plum fleece. Cut a 3 x 26½-in. (8 x 67-cm) strip for the waistband. Cut two pockets from the piece of lilac fleece and repeat Step 4 of the Hoodie.

2 Attach the pockets to the back pant sections as illustrated, carefully topstitching alongside the folded inside edge of the bias binding.

3 To make the number appliqué, following the manufacturer's instructions, back the piece of turquoise fleece with fusible bonding web. Using the template, create and apply the motif to the left front pant (see page 125).

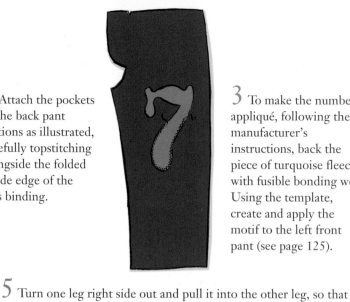

4 With right sides facing, lay the pant fronts on the pant backs and machine stitch the side seams together. Trim the seam allowance to ¼ in. (5 mm). With right sides together, aligning the raw edges, fold the leg sections in half and machine stitch the inner leg seams together. Trim the seam allowance to ¼ in. (5 mm).

5 Turn one leg right side out and pull it into the other leg, so that the right sides are facing. With raw edges aligned, pin, baste (tack), and machine stitch along the curved center seam from the back top edge to the fly front point marked on the pattern piece. Trim the seam allowance on the curve to ¼ in. (5 mm).

6 To create the fake fly front, fold one fly front extension to the inside along the center front line, press the fold, and edge stitch. With right sides facing, lay the outer fly front extension on the inner fly front extension and secure with machine stitches at the upper edges. Using the curved edges as a stitching guide, machine stitch the extensions together through all thicknesses.

7 To make the waistband, machine stitch together the ends of the fabric strip to create a loop. Press open the seam. With right sides facing, pin, baste (tack), and machine stitch the waistband to the upper edge of the pants, matching the waistband seam with the center back seam of the pants.

8 To make the casing for the elastic, fold over 1½ in. (4 cm) of the waistband and press. Matching the top edge of the waistband with its stitched lower edge and the upper edge of the pants, pin, baste (tack), and machine stitch the casing in place, leaving a gap in the stitching to insert elastic. Thread elastic through the casing, adjusting it to fit the waist comfortably. Sew the ends together, push them back into the waistband cavity, and stitch the opening closed. On each pant leg, press the hem ⅝ in. (1.5 cm) to the inside and machine stitch in place.

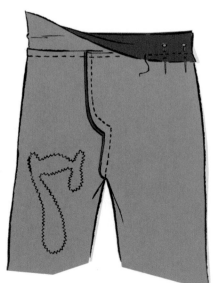

Lucky Seven

Prim and Proper

This charming little shirtdress is as light and fresh as a spring breeze—crisp and neat in classic shirting striped cotton, yet soft and feminine with pretty bound edges in cabbage rose print. It is the perfect choice for a summer bike ride—with or without straw hat—and a style guaranteed to appeal to older girls. Buttons attached with contrast thread provide a dainty finish.

You will need

- Pattern L: front (L1), back (L2), sleeve (L5), and collar (L4)
- Jean pocket templates 1 and 3
- 33-in. (84-cm) piece of 57-in. (145-cm) wide striped fabric
- 140 in. (365 cm) floral bias binding, 1 in. (25 mm) wide
- Seven x 7/8 in. (18 mm) diameter buttons
- Matching thread

Pattern sizes: 12 months, 2 years, **3 years**

Note: Take 3/8-in. (1-cm) seam allowances throughout, unless otherwise stated

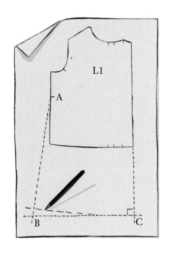

1 The body sections of the shirt pattern require lengthening in order to create a shirtdress. Trace pattern piece L1 and measure 7 1/2 in. (19 cm) down from the bottom of the straight central edge. Re-draw the center line to C. Draw a 12 1/4-in. (31-cm) horizontal line (at a 90° angle) from C to B. Draw a diagonal line from B to A (marked on the pattern piece). Measure 5/8 in. (1.5 cm) along the diagonal line from B to A and from this point re-draw the hemline to C, mirroring the curved hemline of the original shirt pattern. Cut out the paper pattern along the re-drawn lines.

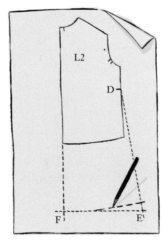

2 Trace pattern piece L2 and measure 7 1/2 in. (19 cm) down from the bottom of the straight central edge. Re-draw the center line to F. Draw a 9-in. (23-cm) horizontal line (at a 90° angle) from F to E. Draw a diagonal line from E to D (marked on the pattern piece). Measure 5/8 in. (1.5 cm) along the diagonal line from E to D and from this point re-draw the hemline to F, mirroring the curved hemline of the original shirt pattern. Cut out the paper pattern along the re-drawn lines.

3 Using the modified pattern pieces together with existing pattern pieces provided, cut two front sections (left and right), one back section, two sleeves, two collars (upper and under), and a 4¾ x 53½-in. (12 x 136-cm) strip for the tie belt. Transfer all pattern markings onto the fabric before removing the paper pattern pieces. Stay stitch the necklines 3/8 in. (1 cm) in from the cut edges to prevent them from stretching.

4 To make the front facings, lay both front sections wrong side up on your work surface. Turn the center front edges 1 1/4 in. (3 cm) to the wrong side, press, and baste (tack) to secure. Turn the center front edges 1 1/4 in. (3 cm) to the right side and pin. Taking one front section, make a 90° angle at the neck edge by stitching from the folded edge to the dot and up to the upper edge. Trim the seam allowance and clip into the stitched corner. Turn the facing right side out and press. Repeat for the other front section.

5 Make seven buttonholes evenly spaced from the top neck toward the bottom edge in the facing of the right front section and put to one side. Cut two 4³/₄-in. (12-cm) squares for the breast pockets and four 6¹/₄-in. (16-cm) squares for the large front and back pockets from the fabric remnants. Bind the upper edge of the six "pocket" squares and the lower edge of the two sleeves with lengths of bias binding (see page 125).

6 Aligning the top edges, place the template on a fabric square and wrap the excess fabric over it, steam pressing flat as you go around the template. Remove the template and trim down the excess to ³/₈ in. (1 cm). Repeat for the remaining small pocket and four large pockets.

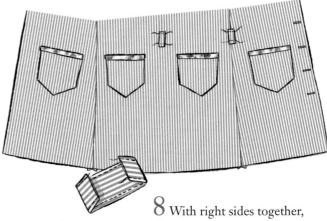

7 Attach the pockets to the front and back sections of the dress, as illustrated, topstitching close to the side and lower edges of the pockets.

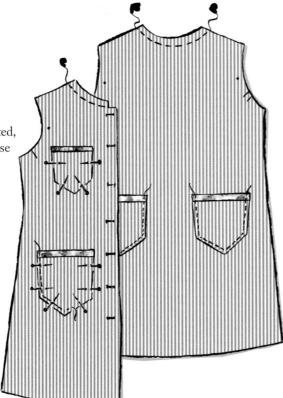

8 With right sides together, stitch the front sections to the back section at the side seams. Press open the seams, open out the shirtdress, and lay it right side up on your work surface. To make the belt loops, fold a 2¹/₄ x 9¹/₂-in. (6 x 24-cm) strip in half along its entire length and press. Open out. Fold both long raw edges ³/₈ in. (1 cm) in toward the middle crease line, press, and fold in half again. Machine stitch along the length of the strip to secure the folds. Cut the strip into three equal lengths and fold under the short ends. Sew the belt loops to the center back and side seams of the dress at waist level.

9 With right sides together, stitch the front sections to the back section at the shoulder seams. Make and attach the collar (see page 123). Using the longest stitch length, machine stitch ³/₈ in. (1 cm) inside and around the sleeve heads between the balance marks in readiness for easing them into the armholes.

10 With right sides together, fold the sleeves lengthwise, align the raw edges, and stitch the underarm seams. Press open the seams. Trim away the 5/8 in. (1.5 cm) hem allowance at the bottom edges of the sleeves. Bind the sleeve edges with lengths of bias binding (see page 125). Attach the sleeves to the shirtdress (see page 123).

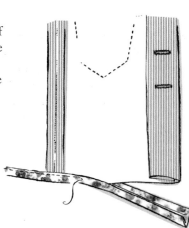

11 Bind the hem of the shirtdress with the remaining length of bias binding along the entire length of the hem, including the bottom edges of the two double-folded front facings.

12 To make the tie belt, pin and baste (tack) a 53 1/2-in. (136-cm) length of bias binding along the entire length of the fabric strip. Edge stitch the binding in place.

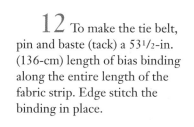

13 With right sides together and aligning the raw edges, machine stitch along the entire length of the strip, leaving a gap in the stitching at the center to turn the belt right side out. Refold the strip so that the long seam runs along the center of the entire length of the belt. Machine the opening at both ends closed. Snip off the corners, turn right side out, and press flat. Edge stitch the belt to finish. Cut open the buttonholes and attach buttons to the front of the shirtdress.

Prim and Proper

Peasant Dreams

This adorable two-piece look is practical as well as stylish. The roomy smock top—so versatile, it goes with everything—and elastic-waisted skirt are easy to slip on and off. The eyelet-edged bib, scoop neck ties, and gently gathered bodice will flatter all sizes, as will the generous cut of the three-tier dirndl. Mix colors, prints, and novel trims together with care, so the final result is eclectic yet harmonious.

To make the tunic

1 Using the pattern pieces provided, cut two front sleeves (left and right), one back (on the fold), one 4½ x 19¾-in. (11 x 50-cm) strip for the upper band at the front, and one 4½ x 14½-in. (11 x 37-cm) strip for the upper band at the back in plain fabric. Cut one 2¾ x 19¾-in. (7 x 50-cm) strip for the lower band at the front, one 2¾ x 14½-in. (7 x 37-cm) strip for the lower band at the back, and two 2¾ x 10-in. (7 x 25-cm) strips for the lower band of the sleeves in contrast plain fabric. In print fabric, cut two bibs using the pattern pieces provided, one 2 x 19¾-in. (5 x 50-cm) strip for the middle band at the front, one 2 x 14½-in. (7 x 37-cm) strip for the middle band at the back, and two 2 x 10-in. (5 x 25-cm) strips for the middle band of the sleeves.

2 Aligning the center fronts, lay the bib paper pattern on top of the wrong side of one fabric bib and carefully transfer the dots to mark the stitching line for the front slit. With right sides facing and aligning all edges, lay the bib pieces together and join the dots with machine stitches. Re-stitch the point to reinforce. Carefully cut the front slit and snip into the corners, avoiding cutting through the machine stitches.

3 Turn the bib pieces wrong sides together and press. Topstitch the front slit and stay stitch ¼ in. (5 mm) in from the edges of the bib to keep them aligned. Attach a 7-in. (18-cm) length of bias binding across the bib front (approximately 1½ in./3.5 cm in from the lower cut edge) and a 6¼-in. (16-cm) length of eyelet trim (broderie anglaise) to the bottom edge, as illustrated.

You will need

For the tunic

- Pattern P: front sleeve (P1), bib (P2), and back bodice (P3)
- 14-in. (36-cm) piece of 45-in. (112-cm) wide plain fabric
- 11-in. (28-cm) piece of 45-in. (112-cm) wide contrast plain fabric
- 11-in. (28-cm) piece of 45-in. (112-cm) wide print fabric
- 78¾ in. (200 cm) eyelet trim (broderie anglaise)
- 118 in. (300 cm) bias binding, ¾ in. (20 mm) wide
- Matching thread

For the skirt

- 15¾-in. (40-cm) piece of 44-in. (112-cm) wide plain fabric
- 13½-in. (34-cm) piece of 44-in. (112-cm) wide stripe fabric
- 19¾-in. (50-cm) piece of 44-in. (112-cm) wide print fabric
- 19 in. (48 cm) elastic, ¾ in. (20 mm) wide
- Matching thread

Pattern sizes: 12 months, 2 years, **3 years**

Note: Take ⅜-in. (1-cm) seam allowances throughout, unless otherwise stated

Peasant Dreams

4 Attach an 8¾-in. (22-cm) length of eyelet trim to the sleeve edge that will be attached to the bib. With right sides together, machine stitch a front sleeve to the bib. Press the seam allowances toward the bib and topstitch along the seam. Repeat for the other sleeve.

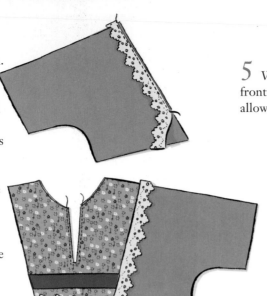

5 With right sides facing and aligning the edges, machine stitch the front and back bodice together at the shoulder seams. Press the seam allowances toward the back bodice and topstitch along the seam.

6 To assemble the decorative sleeve bands, attach a 10-in. (25-cm) length of eyelet trim to the top edge of the lower band in contrast plain fabric. With right sides facing, machine stitch it to the bottom edge of the upper band in print fabric. Press open the seam allowance. Repeat to make the second sleeve band.

7 Lay the completed bodice right side up on your work surface. With right sides together, place a decorative band on top of the bodice sleeve and stitch it in place as illustrated. Repeat for the other sleeve. Stay stitch the necklines ¼ in. (5 mm) in from the cut edges to prevent them from stretching during make. Bind the neck edge in one continuous action with a 53½-in. (136-cm) length of bias binding to form the front neck ties (see page 125).

8 With right sides facing, machine stitch the front and back bodices together at the underarm seams. Press the seams open. Bind each sleeve edge with a 10¼-in. (26-cm) length of bias binding. Put to one side. To make the lower part of the tunic, repeat Steps 6 and 7 using the upper, middle, and lower bands. Once the front and back panels are assembled, with right sides facing, machine stitch them together at the side seams and press the seams open.

9 Gather the center of the top edge of the front upper band, so that the total width is the same as the bottom edge of the bodice (see page 122). With right sides together, attach the gathered lower part of the tunic to the bodice, ensuring that the gathers are evenly placed at the center front. Baste (tack) in place and then machine stitch. Trim the tunic hem with a 33½-in. (85-cm) length of bias binding.

To make the skirt

1 Cut two 6³/₄ x 32¹/₄-in. (17 x 82-cm) plain fabric strips for the upper bands, two 8³/₄ x 32¹/₄-in. (22 x 82-cm) print fabric strips for the middle bands, and two 5¹/₂ x 32¹/₄-in. (14 x 82-cm) striped fabric strips for the "trompe l'oeil petticoat" lower bands. With right sides facing, machine stitch the front and back bands together at the side seams and press open.

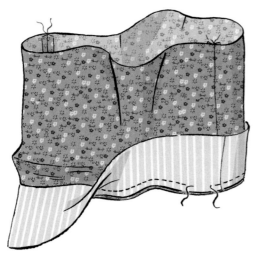

2 Fold the lower band in half lengthwise and press. Turn under 1¹/₂ in. (4 cm) on the bottom edge of the middle band, press in a crease, and open out the fold. With right sides facing, matching the side seams and aligning the raw edges, machine stitch the lower band to the middle band.

3 Re-fold the middle band over onto the lower band and machine stitch through all thicknesses, 1¹/₄ in. (3 cm) in from the edge. With right sides together and matching the side seams, machine stitch the upper band to the middle band.

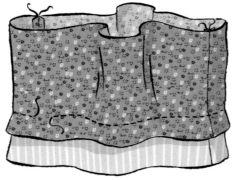

4 To make the casing for the elastic waistband, double hem the top edge by folding over ³/₈ in. (1 cm) and then 1 in. (2.5 cm), and press. Pin, baste (tack), and edge stitch the casing in place, leaving a gap in the stitching to insert elastic. Thread elastic through the casing, adjusting it to fit the waist comfortably. Sew the ends together and stitch the opening closed.

Techniques

Patterns and templates

Transferring patterns

The patterns and templates you need to make the projects in this book are on pull-out sheets at the back. They are all full size, so you do not need to enlarge them. Following the required size, trace the patterns you need, including all markings, onto tissue paper, tracing paper, or pattern paper, and cut them out, cutting along the required line; a $^3/_8$-in. (1-cm) seam allowance (stitching line) is included but not printed on the patterns. Trace any templates that you need, including all markings, onto thin card. Place them on the wrong side of the fabric and draw around them, using tailor's chalk or a "disappearing" fabric marker pen.

Cutting out fabric

Lay your fabric on a flat surface and smooth it out. To cut one fabric piece, place the paper pattern on single-thickness fabric, right side up. To cut "mirror image" left and right fabric pieces, place the paper pattern on double-thickness fabric, folding the fabric with right sides together. To cut one symmetrical fabric piece from a half paper pattern, place the straight, solid outer line of the paper pattern on the fold of the double-thickness fabric, folding the fabric with right sides together. Pin the paper pattern pieces to the fabric and cut along the edge, using sharp fabric scissors.

Balance marks

Short, straight lines at the edges of the pattern indicate points that need to be matched across different pattern pieces.

Transfer them from the paper pattern to the fabric, using tailor's chalk or a "disappearing" fabric marker pen. The simplest solution is to snip the fabric edges, making balance mark "notches." It's also a good idea to notch the end of fold lines and center lines.

Other marks

Dots indicate the position of pockets, buttons, eyelets, and so on, and any areas that require embellishment with embroidery stitches. After cutting, transfer all markings to the wrong side of the fabric before removing the paper pattern. Use pins, tailor's chalk, or a "disappearing" fabric marker pen.

Sewing techniques

Stay stitching

This is a small machine stitch sewn into the seam allowance of a curved edge, approximately $^1/_8$ in. (3 mm) in from the permanent line of stitching, to keep the curve from stretching or distorting.

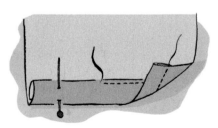

Double hem

Depending on the measurements given in each project, fold the edge of the fabric over to the wrong side and press. Fold over again,

pin, baste (tack), press, and machine stitch in place, stitching as close as possible to the folded edge.

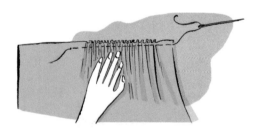

Gathering by hand

With a needle and thread, work running stitches along the edge to be gathered. Gently pull one end of the thread to gather the fabric to the required length, making sure the gathers are even. Secure with a few stitches at the end.

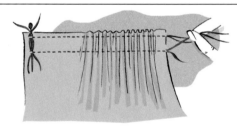

Gathering by machine

Using the longest stitch length, machine stitch two parallel lines $^3/_8$ in. (1 cm) apart along the edge to be gathered. Secure all the threads at one end with a pin and gently pull the two top threads at the other end to gather the fabric to the required length, making sure the gathers are even. Secure these threads with another pin. When attaching the gathered fabric to another fabric piece, use a normal stitch length and machine stitch between the parallel lines of stitching to secure. Remove the parallel lines of stitching to finish.

To set in a sleeve

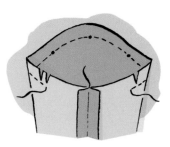 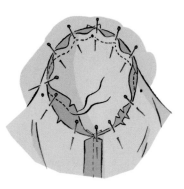 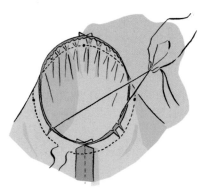

1 Using the longest machine stitch, sew ³/₈ in. (1 cm) inside and around the sleeve head between the balance marks (notches). With right sides facing, machine stitch the sleeve together at the underarm seam and press open.

2 With right sides together, pin the sleeve edge to the armhole edge, matching the underarm seams, sleeve/armhole notches, the center dot on the sleeve with the shoulder seam, and the remaining two dots.

3 Pull the easing stitches so that the sleeve fits the armhole, remembering to distribute the fullness evenly. Pin, baste (tack), and machine stitch the sleeve in place. Carefully remove the easing stitches and shrink out the fullness with a steam iron.

To attach a shirt collar
It is essential that all balance marks (notches) and dots on patterns are transferred to their corresponding fabric pattern pieces.

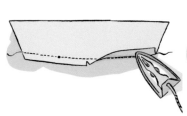 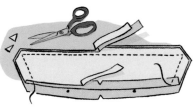 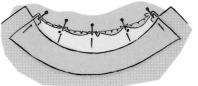 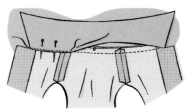

1 Attach iron-on interfacing to the wrong side of the top collar, machine stitch ³/₈ in. (1 cm) in from the notched edge, fold under, and press.

2 With right sides facing, stitch the top collar to the collar facing (under collar), leaving the notched edges open. Trim the seam allowance and snip off the corners. Turn the collar right side out and press.

3 Snip the neck edge of the garment to the stay stitching (as instructed in the project). With right sides together and aligning the raw edges, pin the collar facing to the neck edge of the garment, matching the notches, placing the ends of the collar at the center front of the garment and the dots at the shoulder seams. Machine stitch the collar to the neck edge.

4 Trim the seam allowance, snip the curves, and press the seam allowance toward the inside of the collar. Neatly hand stitch or machine stitch the pressed edge of the top collar over the neck seam.

Techniques

To attach a coat collar

It is essential that all balance marks (notches) and dots on patterns are transferred to their corresponding fabric pattern pieces.

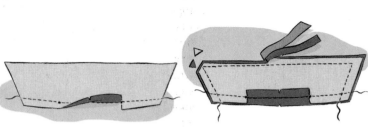

1 Attach iron-on interfacing to the wrong side of the top collar and machine stitch ³/₈ in. (1 cm) in from the notched edge. Snip the notched edge to the machine stitching at the dots and press the seam allowance between the snips, as illustrated.

2 With right sides facing, stitch the top collar to the collar facing (under collar), leaving the notched edges open. Trim the seam allowance, snip off the corners, turn the collar right side out, and press.

3 With right sides together and aligning the raw edges, pin the collar facing to the neck edge of the garment, matching the notches and placing the dots at the shoulder seams. Machine stitch both top collar and facing to the front neck edge as far as the folded-under/pressed edge.

4 Machine stitch the collar facing section only to the remaining section of the neck edge. Once the front facings of the garment have been attached (refer to each individual project), carefully stitch the pressed edge of the top collar over the neck seam.

To make "contour-stitched" patch pockets

1 Fold over the top edge of the pocket to the wrong side by ³/₈ in. (1 cm) and press. With right sides facing, fold over a further ³/₄ in. (2 cm). Holding the fold in place with pins, topstitch around the three remaining raw edges of the pocket along the seam allowance line, using color-matched thread.

2 Snip off the seam allowance at the top corners of the pocket. Turn the folded edge right side out and press.

3 Fold over the remaining seam allowance to the wrong side along the stitched line, neatly pleating and steam pressing the excess fabric as you turn the rounded corners.

Techniques

To shorten a zipper fastener

1 Measure the length of the opening to be fitted with the zipper fastener and mark this length on the zipper tape. Open the zipper and cut the zipper tapes below the stoppers.

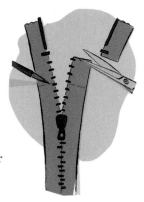

2 For nylon zippers, carefully trim off the teeth above the markings, fold under the trimmed zipper tapes, and sew a small bar on each zipper tape over the first tooth with buttonhole thread.

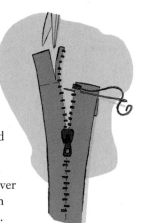

3 For metal zippers, pull the stopper from the zipper tape and retain. Remove the metal teeth above the markings with pliers and re-attach the stoppers above the remaining teeth.

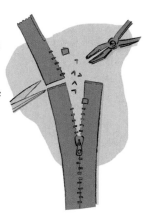

Decorative effects

Bias binding

Fold a length of ready-made bias binding over lengthwise, gently steam-pressing as you fold. Neatly insert the raw edge of the fabric to be bound into the folded binding. Pin, baste (tack), and machine stitch in place. Note: "Shrink" the binding around corners with a steam iron before sewing to avoid puckering.

To make your own binding, cut a length of fabric 2 in. (5 cm) wide on the bias—at an angle of 45° to the selvage. Fold both long edges over to the wrong side so that they meet in the exact center of the strip. Steam press the folds. Aligning the folded edges, re-fold the strip in half, and press again. Attach in the same way as for ready-made bias binding.

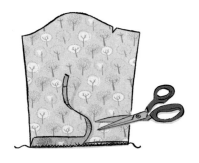

Picot edging

Fold the raw edge of the fabric over to the wrong side by 3/8 in. (1 cm), or as stated. Steam press in a crisp fold. Machine stitch along the edge, using small zigzag stitches, guiding the needle of your sewing machine so that it falls off the fabric, wrapping the threads around the edge. Carefully trim away the seam allowance, taking extra care not to cut the thread.

Appliqué

Trace the appliqué motif onto thin card and cut out. Cut a square of paper-backed fusible bonding web large enough to accommodate the appliqué motif. Lay the square on the wrong side of your appliqué fabric, adhesive side down, and press with a hot iron to heat bond.

1 Place the card template on the paper-backed side of the appliqué fabric and draw around it with a pencil. Carefully cut out the motif and peel away the paper backing.

2 Place the motif, adhesive side down, on the main fabric and press with a hot iron to attach. For a professional finish, machine stitch all around the motif with a small, dense zigzag stitch.

Embroidery stitches

Backstitch
Work from right to left. Bring the needle up at A, down at B, and up again at C. The distance between A and B should be the same as the distance between A and C. To begin the next stitch, insert the needle at A again.

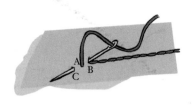

French knot
Bring the needle up from the back of the fabric to the front. Wrap the thread two or three times around the tip of the needle. Reinsert the needle at the point where it first emerged, holding the wrapped threads with the thumbnail of your non-stitching hand, and pull the needle through.

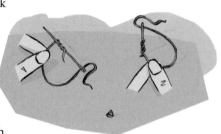

Tassels

1 Cut a square of medium-weight card—the size being equal to the length you want your tassel to be—with a slot inside, 3/4 in. (2 cm) down from the top edge and open at one end. Place a strand of yarn or thread securely across the top edge of the square and start winding yarn vertically round it until you have the desired fullness.

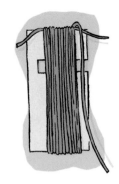

2 Slip another strand of yarn in and out of the slot, wrap it round the wound yarn, and tie securely in a double knot. Tie the strand of yarn at the top of the square in a double knot to secure the top of the wound yarn. Using a pair of sharp scissors, cut the wound yarn at the bottom of the square, slide the tassel off the card, and trim away any uneven ends.

The perfect finish

Pressing seams
Press seams open from the wrong side, unless instructed otherwise. (If you press seams from the right side, you may mark the fabric.) If you are stitching together two pieces that already have seams, press open the first seams, snip off the corners of the seam allowances, and align the seams exactly (if appropriate) when pinning the fabric pieces together.

Trimming seam allowances
To get the best possible shape to collars, cuffs, and waistbands, carefully trim down the seam allowances to about 1/4 in. (5 mm) after stitching.

Snipping corners
Snip diagonally across the seam allowance at corners to eliminate bulk and to achieve neat right angles when the garment is turned right side out.

Finishing curved edges
On curved seams, clip into the seam allowance after stitching, to maintain smooth curves when the garment is turned right side out. For inward curves, cut small slits. For outward curves, cut wedge-shaped notches.

Using pinking shears
Using the saw-toothed blades of pinking shears to trim down seam allowances after stitching not only minimizes fraying of the seam allowances but also provides the notches required for smooth curved seams.

Using your sewing machine
Use the zigzag stitch on your sewing machine—using the maximum stitch width and length—to neaten seam edges and minimize fraying.

Using a serger/overlocker
For a truly professional finish, use an "overlocking" machine, which simultaneously trims and over-edge stitches the seam allowance.

SUPPLIERS

US Suppliers

Amy Butler
www.amybutlerdesign.com

Britex Fabrics
146 Geary Street
San Francisco
CA 94108
415-392 2910
www.britexfabrics.com

Cia's Palette
4155 Grand Ave S.
Minneapolis
MN 55409
612-823 5558
www.ciaspalette.com

Purl Patchwork
147 Sullivan Street
New York
NY 10012
212-420 8798
www.purlsoho.com

Reprodepot Fabrics
413-527 4047
www.reprodepotfabrics.com

Tinsel Trading Company
1 West 37th Street
New York
NY 10018
212-730 1030
www.tinseltrading.com

Z and S Fabrics
681 S. Muddy Creek Road
Denver
PA 17517
www.zandsfabrics.com

UK Suppliers

Borovicks
16 Berwick Street
London W1F 0HP
020 7437 2180
www.borovickfabricsltd.co.uk

The Cloth House
47 Berwick Street
London W1F 8SJ
020 7437 5155
www.clothhouse.com

Cloud Cuckoo Land (vintage clothing)
6 Charlton Place
London N1 8AJ
020 7354 3141

Dreamtime (vintage clothing)
6 Pierrepoint Arcade
Camden Passage
London N1 8EA
07804 261082

John Lewis
Oxford Street
London W1A 1EX
020 7629 7711
www.johnlewis.com

Kleins
5 Noel Street
London W1F 8GD
020 7437 6162
www.kleins.co.uk

Liberty
Regent Street
London W1B 5AH
020 7734 1234
www.liberty.co.uk

Loop
15 Camden Passage
London N1 8EA
020 7288 1160
www.loopknitting.com

MacCulloch & Wallis
25–26 Dering Street
London W1S 1AT
020 7629 0311
www.macculloch-wallis.co.uk

The Make Lounge (courses)
49–51 Barnsbury Street
London N1 1PT
020 7609 0275
www.themakelounge.com

VV Rouleaux
102 Marylebone Lane
London W1U 2QD
020 7224 5179
www.vvrouleaux.com

European Suppliers

Almacenes Cobiàn
Plaza Pontejos, 2
28012 Madrid
Spain
91 522 25 25
www.almacenescobian.es

Les Coupons de Saint-Pierre
2 rue Joseph Sansboeuf
75008 Paris
France
01 42 94 17 12

La Droguerie
9 & 11 rue du Jour
75001 Paris
France
01 45 08 93 27
www.ladroguerie.com

Entrée des Fournisseurs
8 rue des Francs Bourgeois
75003 Paris
France
01 48 87 58 98
www.entreedesfournisseurs.com

Megino
Corredera Alta de San Pablo, 12
28004 Madrid
91 522 64 50
www.megino.net

Le Rouvray
3 rue de la Bûcherie
75005 Paris
01 43 25 00 45
www.lerouvray.com

Tissus Reine
3–5 place Saint-Pierre
75018 Paris
01 46 06 02 31
www.tissus-reine.com

Les Touristes
17 rue des Blancs-Manteaux
75004 Paris
01 42 72 10 84
www.lestouristes.eu

INDEX